"Finally, a guide that tells us the road to happiness is not about money, fame, or success but about something much more fundamental."

Vera Berg, President, Vera Berg and Associates, Institutional Fundraiser

"When I tell people I'm reading a book about the Aristotelian theory of happiness and how it applies in the modern world, their eyes light up and they start asking questions. This book provides a checklist to see if certain actions will be more or less likely to bring real happiness. Looking through the lens of Aristotle's theory, a person can see if their actions will improve their chances for happiness. This book lays out an incredibly simple template for every person regardless of faith, gender, race or any other circumstance to systematically improve their chances for acting in a virtuous way and lead a happier life. It's not often you can read secular words written more than two thousand years ago that give you a definitive step-by-step instruction to happiness. This is a very important book."

Scott Grove, President, Auto Road Services Inc.

"This book applies Aristotelian theory to everyday life with insight and allows readers to understand the philosophical underpinnings of the means to a satisfying existence."

John Cox, President, Cape Cod Community College

"It's amazing how calling on the universal wisdom of an ancient philosopher—Aristotle—can help guide an individual in these turbulent times to lead a better, happier life. Every chapter caused me to reflect on how I have conducted my life, how I could do better, and thus become a better person—a happier person. It's clearly written, yet provocative, and the simple message is brought home in various situations: do the right thing, for the right reason, to the right person, at the right time."

Alan Rothenberg, Bank Founder, Chairman

"The authors have paved the road to happiness with simplicity. Choosing one of the world's greatest thinkers of all time to guide us, the authors make doing "the right thing for the right person at the right time for the right reason" a practical way to live. With its use of everyday examples and identifying *stoppers* that hinder us, this book is a *must read* for anyone who is stuck in finding the true meaning of happiness."

Dave Wilson, Retired National Football League Quarterback

FINDING HAPPINESS
with Aristotle as Your Guide

Action Strategies Based on 10 Timeless Ideas

Gary Madvin and
Geraldine Markel, PhD

iUniverse, Inc.
Bloomington

Finding Happiness with Aristotle as Your Guide
Action Strategies Based on 10 Timeless Ideas

iUniverse books may be ordered through booksellers or by contacting:

iUniverse
1663 Liberty Drive
Bloomington, IN 47403
www.iuniverse.com
1-800-Authors (1-800-288-4677)

Cover Design: John Sturgeon Designs, Ann Arbor, MI

ISBN: 978-1-4620-6123-5 (sc)
ISBN: 978-1-4620-6126-6 (hc)
ISBN: 978-1-4620-6125-9 (e)

Printed in the United States of America

iUniverse rev. date: 05/22/2012

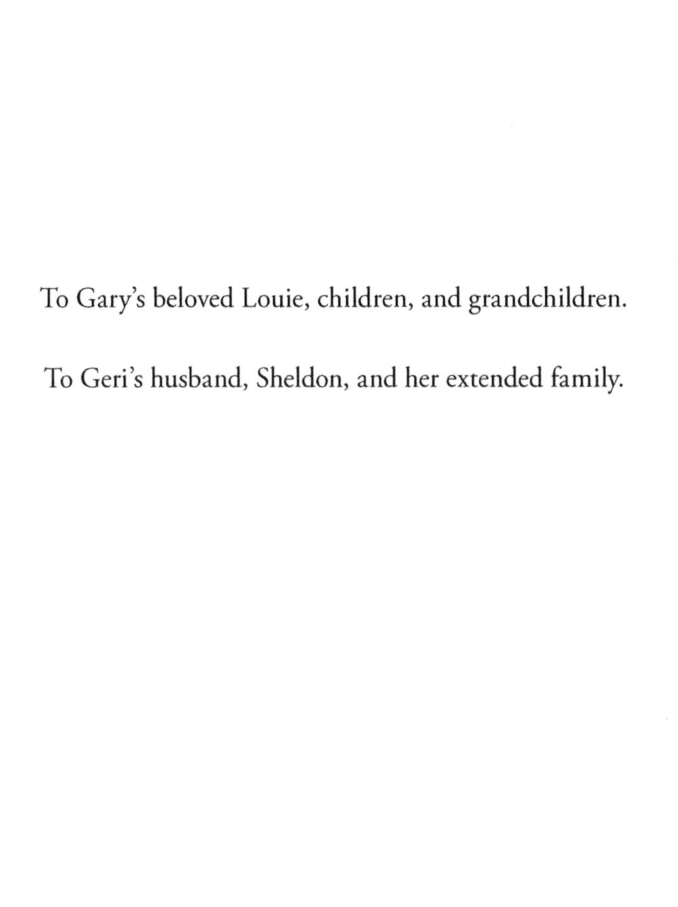

To Gary's beloved Louie, children, and grandchildren.

To Geri's husband, Sheldon, and her extended family.

Acknowledgments

The completion of this book resulted from the help of a number of people. We are particularly grateful for the help received from people who took the time to read the first drafts of the manuscript and provided comments and insights about possible changes. Our readers included Mike Bain, Vera Berg, Beth Cox, Patrick Davidson, Paul Devore, Jack Dulworth, Scott Grove, Brent Guttman, Nan Halperin, Mark Kruspodin, Barbara Madvin, Jeremy Madvin, Richard Papasian, Alan Rothenberg, Steve Sanett, John Shannahan, Carmen Visser, David Wilson, and Deanna Wolfire. They deserve special thanks. An additional thank you goes to Barbara Madvin for her tireless efforts at organizing and reformatting the manuscript.

We are especially indebted to the professional contributions of Barbara McNichol of Barbara McNichol Editorial. She provided the perfect blend of expertise, patience, and creativity. Always prompt and efficient, her attention to detail and clarity was a major contribution.

Special appreciation goes to our spouses. Louie helped Gary from the time he first started graduate school through the completion of his thesis and all of the difficulties in finishing this book. Shel has supported all of Geri's professional endeavors for many decades.

Contents

Preface

Why do two professionals from the different areas of business and educational psychology want to apply the ideas of a Greek philosopher born twenty-four centuries ago to your life in this century?

The following journeys of Gary and Geri reveal the origins of their interest in Aristotle's view of happiness—and what their discoveries can mean to you.

Gary's Journey

"My interest began with a stint as a door-to-door vacuum cleaner salesman while working my way through college. Our group sold high-priced vacuum cleaners to vulnerable people who signed contracts without understanding what they were buying—not much different from the way mortgages were sold and securitized in the years before the 2008 financial crisis. Dissatisfied mortgage customers have had to deal with a mess. Similarly, the vacuum cleaner people I worked for had no qualms about cheating their customers or taking advantage of them. I was part of that system while simultaneously pursuing 'the greater good' through a teaching career. At the age of twenty, worried about how to reconcile these two worlds, I reached an ethical crossroads, quit this job, and chose 'the greater good.'

"After graduating from Wayne State University in Detroit, Michigan, I become a high school history teacher in schools located on the mean streets of southeast Detroit. Eventually, I became a life insurance salesman, a philosophy graduate student (specializing in Aristotle's ethics), and the founder of a large financial planning company servicing wealthy people. Along the way, I discovered that, regardless of their prominence or wealth, most of the people I met struggled to find satisfaction and happiness. This gave birth to the ideas you'll read about in this book.

"When I first thought about how to achieve happiness, I presumed that, if you met your career and family goals, then happiness would follow. As it turned out, many of the people I encountered felt unhappy even though they led highly enviable lives—or so it seemed. Through experience and the study of philosophy, I realized that—no matter what their circumstances— people tend to establish obstacles—what we call *stoppers*—to their own happiness. While each person's story sounds different, the *unhappiness* factor for many sounds the same. It's expressed in comments like 'I'd be happy if I'd chosen a different profession' or 'I'd be happy if my spouse paid more attention to me' or 'I'd be happy if I had more money.' Presumably, if they solve one or two problems, they'll be problem-free and therefore happy.

"Yet people don't achieve happiness via external success, I've come to realize. Messages about 'the good life' that most parents and teachers convey simply aren't true. Knowing this compelled me to seek the truth of happiness—to figure out how to achieve an authentically happy life for myself while helping my financial services clients deal with their dissatisfaction.

"So to pursue these goals, I enrolled in a second undergraduate program in philosophy. There, I worked with an assistant professor at UCLA who introduced me to Aristotle's views on happiness. After three years of study, I entered a masters program at California State

University, Los Angeles, which I completed by writing my thesis titled *The Possibility of Using Philosophy as a Tool for Happiness*. Since then, I've felt compelled to combine my knowledge of Aristotle's philosophy with my business experience to help others gain greater happiness and life satisfaction. Writing this book has been a critical part of my journey."

Geri's Journey

"My journey began as a middle school teacher in a working-class community in Bellville, Michigan. Later, I was a substitute teacher in a rough Staten Island high school and subsequently a reading consultant, special educator, training consultant, and university faculty member. Regardless of my position, though, I saw my role as helping others improve performance and productivity—achievements that supposedly would pave the way to happiness and satisfaction.

"Today, as an educational psychologist who coaches and speaks, I train others to manage their minds so they can achieve their goals. My clients learn strategies and develop skills to accomplish what they want—whether they take business/industry training programs or they receive counseling for ADD and/or learning disabilities. As a result of our work together, they learn to fulfill their responsibilities faster, better, and with less stress.

"In spite of achieving their goals, though, I observed that many of them don't experience a sense of peace or sustained satisfaction. Yes, research-based strategies can help people improve their skills and enhance their confidence, but ensuring happiness isn't part of the package.

"I realized that many in the fields of education, training, and mental health put an emphasis on psychology (the way emotions influence behavior) rather than philosophy (how attitudes, assumptions, and logic influence action). So I began focusing on rational thought as part of my cognitive behavioral psychology studies, enhanced by exploring contemporary ethics and values with Gary, my cousin through marriage. As members of a large family, Gary and I spent copious hours during vacations discussing our experiences and insights. For me, the value lay in how Gary integrated philosophical thought with his own interpretations and perspective. The result? Seemingly complex issues became clear and problems became more solvable. In turn, Gary benefited from my expertise in training, motivating, and activating others to achieve their goals.

"As Gary set out to share his understanding of Aristotle's philosophy with a larger community, we decided to develop a self-help guide to help people apply Aristotle's principles to everyday life. Including both insights and activities, it contributes to the search for happiness in a valuable, practical way.

"My challenge became designing ways to get readers like you involved in an active rather than passive manner. As you read this guide, you'll find the discussion questions and other activities will move you to a deeper level of understanding.

"Gary and I sincerely hope that, by applying Aristotle's ideas to your everyday living, you'll achieve the happiness you seek in your life."

Gary Madvin (garymadvin@happinesswitharistotle.com)
Geraldine Markel, PhD (gerimarkel@happinesswitharistotle.com)
2012

"The good of man is an activity of the soul in conformance with excellence or virtue."
—Aristotle (*Nichomachean Ethics* 1098a15)

Introduction

Just how happy are people in the United States? According to several surveys by the Pew Research Center (2006), only a third of adults in this country say they are *very happy*. According to a Gallup survey, fewer than half of the Americans surveyed reported they have "a lot of happiness/enjoyment without a lot of stress/worry" (Witters, 2010).

What about you?

- Do you think happiness is eluding you?
- Have you ever thought about changing your life to achieve greater happiness?
- Do you feel discontent in the midst of plenty?
- Do you know what *stops* you from attaining happiness?

This book introduces ancient philosophical principles about happiness into your modern-day life. You'll discover that Aristotle's ideas provide tools for defining happiness as well as identifying attitudes and behaviors that increase contentment and well-being.

Aristotle has reputedly formulated one of the most meaningful commentaries about happiness. The ways he addresses issues bring a depth that is just as important today as in ancient times. Best of all, putting Aristotle's ideas into action can contribute to a life plan that leads to your own happiness.

As you know, life presents a myriad of problems, especially in turbulent times. Whatever your troubles, though, the way you think and act in response to them can determine whether you attain happiness. Aristotle's advice provides a prescription for the correct way of thinking and acting based on rational decision making. He said that happiness naturally results from leading your life in a particular way—*not* from high productivity or great accomplishment.

Ivory Tower View of Philosophy

Many people believe it's foolish to think philosophy can help them function in the "real" world—a belief derived from the misconception that philosophy belongs solely to the ivory tower of a university. As this misconception goes, philosophy cannot and should not be expected to assist in managing daily living.

Yes, there can be elements of truth to the concept that philosophy isn't useful in daily living. After all, the study of philosophy is pursued mostly in isolated, protected institutions of higher learning. In addition, difficulties abound in clearly explaining a philosopher's view and then converting it for use in the real world. For example, why would Aristotle (or anyone else) think the meaning of people's happiness is anything other than a matter of personal opinion? And isn't it difficult to understand and/or accept the distinction between a *happy* life and a *successful* life? As Aristotle has pointed out, precision isn't possible when applied to subjects like happiness.

Why do so few authors attempt to connect these two worlds? Because it's extremely difficult to link daily experiences to technical philosophical thought. Nevertheless, the chapters here address common problems and ethical issues such as mortality, success and failure, lying and truth telling. The book as a whole turns Aristotle's theory into an action guide for thinking and acting in ways that will enhance your happiness.

Of course, many brilliant thinkers have also written about the meaning of happiness. This book doesn't attempt to compete with them. Rather, it establishes a useful link between great philosophical thought and daily life. To that end, you'll read about basic tenets of Aristotle with extensions, interpretations, and applications from Madvin, Markel, and others. For instance, the ideas of Layers and Channels and a Wall of Happiness developed by Madvin are tied to—and meant to extend—Aristotle's philosophy.

No matter the source of a particular idea, the more you discuss and apply Aristotle's ideas to your life, the easier you can move toward a deeper, more satisfying experience of happiness.

Why Turn to Aristotle?

Aristotle lived from 382 to 322 BCE as one of the most influential philosophers of all time. Until the seventeenth century in Europe, he was viewed as the main authority on almost everything outside of religion. He wrote penetrating analyses on a vast range of topics, establishing him as a strong focal point for many current disciplines.

Aristotle contributed an essential and powerful definition of happiness. As Ackrill noted in his book *Aristotle the Philosopher* (Ackrill, 1981, p. 135), in Aristotle's first book of the *Nicomachean Ethics,* the philosopher brought to the fore various candidates for the title "best life for man"—e.g., the life of pleasure, the life of practical activity, the philosopher's life. In addition, he drew attention to characteristics humans would look for in the ideal life—e.g., entirely satisfying, incapable of improvement, not subject to upset by external misfortunes.

Ackrill's discussion of Aristotle's material pinpointed some of the issue's complexity. As Ackrill commented, "A man is a highly complicated animal with a variety of needs and aims, some of which are subordinate to others. A life-ideal will be a complex goal, not a simple one; it will have some kind of structure" (Ackrill, 1981, p. 135).

Ackrill noted Aristotle's development as a teacher and guide. As a seventeen-year-old youth, Aristotle went to Athens where he entered Plato's Academy and, after his studies, taught for more than twenty years. His master, Plato, is said to have surnamed Aristotle "The Intellect." Aristotle later went to Macedonia to supervise the education of a thirteen-year-old boy who later became Alexander the Great.

In 334 BCE, Aristotle returned to Athens to establish his own school, located in a gymnasium called the Lyceum. This school included a campus, a chapel, classrooms, covered walkways, and shaded gardens. By custom, he taught by conversing with his pupils while walking along the shady lanes of the garden. Alexander the Great, for one, was grateful for this education. In appreciation, he supplied his master with the financial means to form a library and assemble a museum of natural history that Aristotle used to enrich his school. As it developed, the Lyceum contained the Western world's first great library, a museum of natural history, and a zoological garden.

Aristotle sought to develop an empirically sound and rationally coherent worldview that would provide unity and consistency to the whole of life. His intent? It would serve as a model for interpreting and evaluating the human experience, including the timeless topic of happiness. Although written more than two thousand years ago, his messages about happiness can help people deal with the problems of today just as they helped people in ancient times.

Happiness Defined

A definition of happiness in the dictionary describes it as good fortune, joy, a state of well-being or contentment, and optimism. Within this definition are external factors such as good fortune mixed with internal qualities such as feelings of joy, competence, or optimism.

A psychologist's definition of happiness that combines feelings and activities provides a similar description. For example, from the Positive Psychology perspective described by Seligman (Seligman, 1991; 2002; 2011), the definition of happiness includes satisfaction as well as positive actions. More currently, Seligman described happiness as well-being (Seligman, 2010, p. 16), with the goal of Positive Psychology "to increase the amount of *flourishing* in your own life and on the planet" (Seligman, 2010, p. 26). In this definition, the activities in which one engages must be significant.

In the spiritual domain, the Dalai Lama proposed this: "Happiness is determined more by the state of one's mind than by one's external conditions at least once one's basic survival needs are met. You have feelings of peace and contentment and you manifest this state of mind by having compassion toward others" (Lama and Cutler 2009, p. 19). Other leaders, such as Mahatma Gandhi, the Indian political and spiritual leader, suggested that happiness occurs when you experience harmony in what you think, what you say, and what you do (Gandhi, 1993, p. 106).

Many of these definitions have roots in the teachings of Aristotle, whose discussion of happiness provides the basis of this book because of his broad, deep analysis of the topic. Using Aristotle's philosophy, happiness is comprised of knowing the right thing to do, at the right time, and in the right way—and making a conscious decision to act. When we manage our thoughts and actions to attain this goal, then we live satisfied and happy lives.

Stories You'll Find

To show the practical use of Aristotle's thoughts in this book, you'll read stories about people dealing with common dilemmas in contemporary life. These stories flow from day-to-day experiences, mostly from people in the insurance/financial services industry.

However, the profession, gender, or status portrayed doesn't limit a story's meaning to any particular group; the concepts are universal.

Many of the stories describe people you'd imagine would be happy but aren't. They show how Aristotle's philosophy can actually predict such difficulties—and how his guidelines can help you avoid similar situations, thereby setting the stage for your own happiness.

Other stories describe people who appear perfectly happy. Although they experience common problems, they tend to follow (intuitively or by design) principles similar to those embedded in Aristotle's theory. Consistent with Aristotle's theory, for them, happiness is complete and permanent; it never gets higher or better.

As in any writing, personal stories heighten awareness, understanding, and insight. But more than that, the concepts within them provide opportunities to discuss, personalize, and apply these qualities.

What are *Stoppers*?

Can you identify the barriers that stop you from following sage advice? These barriers—labeled *stoppers* in this book—connect the philosophy noted in early chapters with issues of everyday life described in later chapters. *Stoppers* are actions taken or emotions felt that are inconsistent with Aristotle's ideas about achieving happiness. *Stoppers* can put you on the wrong path and/or stop your progress toward living a happy life. You'll find common *stoppers* listed in Chapter 1, discussed in the chapters, and summarized in Appendix I.

Do the Activities to Gain Better Results

To break old habits that will decrease your vulnerability to *stoppers,* you need time and engagement to face issues of significance and consider various options for improving your situation. For this reason, chapters 1 to 8 feature activities for applying the wisdom of Aristotle to your life. You'll find questions and exercises including:

- Points to think about
- Dos and don'ts
- A call to action

As you complete these activities in the eight chapters and four appendixes, you're creating a diary of thoughts that will move you toward a greater understanding of how to achieve happiness in your life. Once you've completed them, you'll have a record of your own journey—and a personalized action guide for living with happiness for the rest of your life. Use the book club guide to extend learning (p. 144).

What to Expect from *Finding Happiness*

The chapters in this book describe and illustrate basic tenets of Aristotle's philosophy, tools from the trenches of the business world, and the barriers (*stoppers*) that people confront and can overcome with the use of Aristotle's ideas. The appendixes feature activities that will change your undesired habits. The following provides a summary.

Chapter 1: "Happiness" describes Aristotle's meaning of happiness, why this meaning is not a matter of opinion, and what is required to achieve a happy life. It also provides Aristotle's definitions of true intelligence and excellence, the role of emotions in the quest for happiness, and the universality of the pursuit of happiness.

Chapter 2: "Responsibility" shows how taking responsibility for your actions moves you toward happiness. Conversely, the denial of responsibility stops you from solving problems and reduces your efforts toward happiness. It discusses the roles played by luck and lying in the pursuit of happiness and how the fear of the truth stops your progress toward happiness.

Chapter 3: "Fame and Fortune" describes the limitations of material success and the error that people commonly make in the pursuit of one dominant end. It addresses the concepts of power and happiness as well as honor.

Chapter 4: "Balance" provides details about the meaning and importance of finding balance in your life as well as Aristotle's tool for deciding how to determine the right balance. You'll discover how seeking the "mean" involves avoiding both excess and deficiency but does not refer to only seeking a compromise.

Chapter 5: "Unrealistic Expectations" shows the ways being unrealistic lead to unhappiness and how to eliminate these expectations from your life. Unrealistic expectations are significant *stoppers* to your pursuit of happiness.

Chapter 6: "Change and Failure" explains why the way you view and handle possible change and potential failure can help or impede happiness. It discusses optimism, negative clues, and ways to reframe your views to reduce this *stopper*.

Chapter 7: "Irresolvable Problems" points out the importance of acknowledging irresolvable problems, particularly your mortality, and how understanding improves the possibility of excellence and happiness. Its discussions pertain to difficult permanent relationships and financial crises.

Chapter 8: "Steps toward Happiness" describes how to organize the major aspects of your life and avoid piling your challenges on top of one another. Ultimately, it will improve your focus and effectiveness in your pursuit of happiness.

Appendix I: "Summary of Ideas and Related Actions, *Stoppers*, and Strategies" provides specific ways to keep the *stoppers* from thwarting your attempts to find happiness. It explains how each strategy reduces the chances of becoming overwhelmed and increases your motivation to do the right thing, at the right time, for the right person, and in the right way—thus adapting Aristotle's guidelines to your daily life.

Appendix II: "Applying the Ideas to Life Dilemmas" provides situations and dilemmas related to each chapter. It challenges you to consider ways to do the right thing, for the right person, at the right time, and for the right reason.

Appendix III: "Applying the Ideas as Your Personal Action Guide" provides charts and activities for using these ideas in your life. It features activities for reflecting on and recording your views or reactions to past, present, and future situations.

Appendix IV: "Discussion Questions or Book Club Guide" provides questions for each chapter that can be used to further discussions of the concepts in a group.

Overall Goal of *Finding Happiness*

What is happiness and how do you view it? This book begins with these questions and opens the door to understanding how Aristotle's ideas and practical suggestions can help you find greater life satisfaction. By the time you've worked through its chapters and appendixes, perhaps you'll conclude that Aristotle was the first and most thoughtful life coach who ever lived!

"Happiness then is the best, noblest, and
most pleasant thing in the world."
—Aristotle (*NE* 1099a24)

Chapter 1: Happiness

Bob retired at the age of thirty-seven after achieving everything he'd dreamed about. He'd made a lot of money in his real estate development business and believed those funds would provide happiness for him and his family. Because Bob had no interest in taking additional financial risk or working as hard as before, he closed his business. During the first year of his retirement, he played a lot of golf at a country club with old friends. Predictably, he got bored with golf and wanted to do something more productive and interesting. Because he'd come from humble beginnings, Bob appreciated his good fortune. Nevertheless, he felt unhappy with his life in retirement, saying, "If I had the chance, I would be glad to give up much of what I've accumulated for a more meaningful life."

Aristotle's philosophy helps explain why Bob's unhappiness could be predicted. Aristotle wouldn't find anything unusual about Bob's desire to find happiness; indeed, most people agree that everyone wants to be happy. However, as Aristotle has pointed out, although people generally agree that everyone wants to be happy, they don't agree about *what happiness is* or *how to achieve it*. It seems that the pursuit of happiness—like anything else—will likely fail if it starts with a faulty plan based on a flawed assumption.

Bob's situation exemplifies that kind of thinking. His unhappiness resulted from acting on a flawed idea. He incorrectly believed that if he didn't have to work, feelings of happiness would naturally follow. Yet he failed to consider the potential *stoppers*—all the thoughts and actions that prevent a person from achieving happiness. As a result, happiness eluded him.

So while Bob appears to be leading the "good life" complete with good reasons to feel happy, he simply doesn't feel satisfied.

Happiness is Not a Matter of Opinion

When describing the meaning of happiness—one of the first items Aristotle discussed in *Nichomachean Ethics* written in 350 BCE—the same people say different things at different times. It appears that their opinions depend on their personal situation at the time they're asked.

For instance, when people who have lots of money get sick, they'll say, "If I have my health, that's all that counts." Yet, when they're sick, many of these people would gladly give up their worldly possessions in return for getting well. But when their health returns, they can easily go back to thinking that money tops the list of importance. Of course, that thinking could be reversed if they become ill again.

Others pinpoint fame as most important, saying, "If only I were famous, I would be happy." But if they become famous and then get ill, they'd give up their fame to get well. This holds true even in matters of lesser importance. People might think they'd be happier if they played golf more, traveled more, or saw their grandchildren more. What's the fallacy in that kind of thinking? That achieving a particular solution to a particular perceived shortcoming will bring them happiness.

No Agreement on Its Definition

At first, it might seem strange that people can change their minds so quickly about this issue. It becomes easier to understand knowing the cause of the vacillation is not having an agreed-upon meaning of happiness.

This lack of agreement leads to a shaky intellectual commitment about what's important at any particular moment. As circumstances change, opinions change. After all, if you're on your deathbed, it's easy to understand why you might give up all your money to get better. What do you have to lose? Yet once you're better, you want that money back in your pocket.

In addition, even if a single theory would help people eliminate the uncertainty, why accept Aristotle's ideas? Moreover, who can blame them for being skeptical about any theory? After all, does any one set of ideas—Aristotle's or anyone else's—apply to everyone in every circumstance? No. Therefore, it seems simple-minded to accept any one particular opinion about happiness.

A theory of happiness needs to fit the reality of numerous variables—different personalities, situations, and opinions—that can vary wildly from one another. Some people say, for example, that happiness is having fun, whether it's playing golf, hiking, having sex, or another activity. Nothing matters, some people say, as long as you're leading your life in a way you claim makes you happy.

Other people say that happiness doesn't require any fun at all, that they'd be happy if they became rich or famous. Still, others say that happiness hinges on having power over people. Clearly, myriad opinions exist. However, only one thing is certain: if you regard every opinion (including your own) as having equal value, you're obligated to try one thing and then another and then still another until (you hope) something works.

Aristotle offers a rational, universal approach to achieving happiness that can be good for all. It's well known that as a historically credible, sound, reasonable source, Aristotle ranks as one of the best. Consider these comments about happiness made by Aristotle:

- There is no goal that can be higher or better than happiness.
- Happiness is complete unto itself and requires no additional features or benefits.
- Nothing can make happiness better; it can't be improved upon.
- Achieving happiness is built on lesser goals that are necessary to reach the happiness objective.

Happiness through Virtuous Living

Aristotle defines virtue as a praiseworthy state of character or mind and soul. He stated, "The happy man will be happy throughout his life; for always, or by preference to everything else, he will be engaged in virtuous action" (*NE* 1100b18).

Most people would say a morally virtuous person strives to do the right thing—

- for the right person
- at the right time
- in the right way
- for the right reason

According to Aristotle, this kind of person has the best chance to be happy. No, he's not recommending a good-natured, passive approach, rather that you *do* something to reach a state of happiness. For example, you can't be considered happy if you're in a coma or a meditative state and can't take action. Thus with no action, you cannot reach the sense of satisfaction necessary for happiness.

Happiness is an Absolute

Aristotle described happiness this way: "We call final without qualification that which is always desirable in itself and never for the sake of something else" (*NE* 1097a30). In other words, if you are already happy, there is nothing that can make you happier. This is because happiness is good unto itself. And because happiness is unconditionally complete in itself—an absolute—once a person is happy, he or she cannot improve his or her "happiness condition."

Is there an additive element to happiness? That is, if people are happy, could improving a situation enable them to be happier still? No. All happy people are similar in their happiness with no additional happiness to be found. The comparatives *happy*, *happier*, and *happiest* simply don't exist. Once you reach happiness, there is nothing else to add.

Aristotle's View of Intelligence

In everyday language, when people are intelligent, it means they have the ability to learn complex sets of facts, respond to new situations, or act shrewdly. Scientists, businesspeople, and those in the professions and arts are examples of intelligent people. Why? Because they show they're able to master knowledge and apply it wisely. Most of the people described in this book would fit this definition of intelligence.

However, Aristotle defines intelligence differently. He said, "Practical wisdom is concerned with things human and things about which it possible to deliberate; for we say this is above all the work of the man of practical wisdom, to deliberate well, but no one deliberates about things invariable, nor about things which have not an end" (*NE* 1141b9). In his view, intelligence isn't about learning facts and understanding concepts; it's about thinking correctly when it comes to practical issues. Intelligence is the quality that allows people to be comfortable with the uncertainties of life. As a result, they're able to decide the right thing to do in circumstances that lack clarity.

An intelligent person, according to Aristotle, has the ability to think about what promotes living well, not only about specific subjects but with a general or global perspective. Possessing practical wisdom, an intelligent person can figure out what's good for human beings and, in a rational way, decide the right action to take in particular situations. Said Aristotle, "Practical wisdom, then, must be a reasoned and true state of capacity to act with regard to human goods" (*NE* 1140b20).

This means people who are shrewd don't meet Aristotle's definition of intelligence because, although they might be thoughtful about their own self-interest, they don't show thoughtfulness about the people around them. As he said, "It is for this reason that we think Pericles and men like him have practical wisdom [intelligence], because they can see what is good for themselves and what is *good for men in general*" [italics added] (*NE* 1140b8).

Aristotle's View of Excellence (Virtue)

Although it's important to give proper credit to *intelligent* people for knowing what to do, that doesn't mean an intelligent person is necessarily an *excellent* person. That person could have the intelligence needed to *know* the right thing to do but lack excellence per se because he or she cannot *do* the right thing. This might be due to a lack of discipline or an irresistible attraction to instant rewards, among other possibilities. Thus, when an intelligent person can see and then *do* the right action, he or she attains *excellence* (virtue).

Excellence, according to Aristotle, is comprised of certain feelings and ways of performing actions—that is, doing the right thing, for the right person, at the right time, and in the right way. That means excellent people don't get seduced by pleasant activities in the moment when the right thing needs to be done (*NE* 1109b5).

Multiple Ends Lead to Wall of Happiness

In Aristotle's view, happiness—the highest of all ends—rests on many more particular ends or results, each an end in itself. People reach happiness, therefore, by reaching a multiplicity of ends (*NE* 1097b21). Some of these ends are family, friends, education, and financial well-being as well as whatever else is pursued. Each of these ends reveals part of who a person is and what he or she does. Therefore, while the *highest* good that can be achieved is happiness, this *ultimate* good is built on a series of lesser goods. To give an analogy, just as bricks build a wall, lesser goods build an ultimate good.

Metaphorically speaking, each activity in one's life is a brick that, in combination with other bricks, makes a wall. Finishing your "wall of happiness" is a self-sufficient end—the highest goal, the final goal, the ultimate good. You know it's come into being because of the combination of lesser self-sufficient ends along the way. Your bricks are ends based on what you value in life (family, friends, health, profession or career, and so on). Each of your "life components" represents an important brick in your wall of life. But only in combination, not individually, do they build a wall. Indeed, each brick is subordinate to the wall.

Stoppers to Happiness

A variety of common barriers can function as *stoppers* to achieving happiness. That is, certain actions, ideas, and/or thoughts can block you from doing the right thing, for the right person, at the right time, and for the right reason. Possible actions, ideas, and/or thoughts include:

- Misunderstanding the true nature of happiness as described by Aristotle.

- Over-relying on emotions, rather than rational thought, when making decisions.
- Lying or denying responsibility to avoid any negative consequences of your actions.
- Overemphasizing the importance of honors, winning, and material goods.
- Not thinking through what's too much and what's not enough when deciding which action to take.
- Having unrealistic expectations—for example, expecting others will reciprocate; believing life's purpose is fun and leisure.
- Resisting inevitable life changes—for example, denying apparent clues; not dealing well with failure.
- Shying away from irresolvable problems—for example, being overwhelmed with emotions long after a crisis or tragedy; forgetting that happiness is attainable even in the worst of times.
- Ignoring (knowingly or unknowingly) the kind of conscious thought and action required to live a happy life.

Aristotle's View of Emotions

Taking Aristotle's view further, although intelligence involves reason, part of the human mind operates from emotion independently from reason. Aristotle observes that when emotions take charge, people don't think or act rationally. Using military terms to compare emotions and reasoning, one's ability to reason is the *general* while one's emotions are the *lieutenants.*

A lieutenant in the army must obey the orders of the general who's in charge. The general must make decisions free of emotion while the lieutenants must carry out the general's orders. Thus, subordinating your emotions to reason allows you to do what's necessary for excellence.

Consider the following line of thinking:

- Reason is required for intelligence.
- Intelligence is required for excellence.
- Excellence is the same as virtue.
- Virtuous activity is required for happiness.

If you base your behavior on these statements, it follows that you must control your emotions to optimize your chances for happiness. If you allow your emotions to rule, you're creating a *stopper* to happiness. Please realize this doesn't mean you make decisions with no emotion attached—something that's both impossible and undesirable. It means thinking rationally about what actions you have to take under current circumstances.

For example, suppose you see a car on fire. In it is a man who can't open the door to get out. Of course, you'd react emotionally—with fear, anxiety, panic. Nevertheless, the man in danger would want you to *think rationally* about the best way to open the door so he can get out. Rational thinking offers the best chance for a positive result.

That's what is meant by basing key life decisions on reason rather emotion. A greater chance for happiness results. And by using reason, you won't encounter as many *stoppers* in pursuing that happiness.

Universality

Says Brenda, a forty-year-old, full-time homemaker who cares for her two children, "I can't see how a discussion about the happiness of privileged businessmen has anything to do with me. Nothing about my life corresponds to their lives. I spend my life taking care of others. I don't have the option of playing golf or traveling around the world going to conferences. I always wanted to have a family, but I wonder sometimes if I made the right choices."

Brenda's point is that her life differs so radically from Bob's that any comparisons simply aren't valid. She takes care of the household and their children and helps her husband with issues that come his way. She doesn't go to conferences or talk in business lingo. Comparing her to Bob borders on the ridiculous in her mind.

Although Brenda's and Bob's life situations are different, at the same time, their ability to pursue happiness is the same. Gender and personal circumstances are *irrelevant* to finding happiness—a universal phenomenon that's the same for everyone.

Follow this example: People live their lives in one life system or another—as full-time homemakers or as firefighters. Some are homemakers during one time in their lives and firefighters at another period. Some are homemakers during the week and firefighters on the weekend. It's easy to believe, as Brenda's comments indicate, that those in different life situations pursue happiness in different ways. Not so. People want to find a good and happy life, despite their financial, social, or demographic status. That means both Brenda and Bob have to use their *intellect* to choose what actions to take in the pursuit of their individual happiness.

Thinking that what you want differs from what others want is clearly a *stopper*. Remember, happiness comes from doing the right thing, for the right person, at the right time, for the right reason. This applies to Brenda, Bob, and the rest of us as well.

Aristotle's ideas provide substantial guidelines for everyone because it's based on a universal ethical value that, by definition, applies to all—without exception. The question that remains is this: "What should you *do* to achieve happiness?"

Living a Happy Life

Happy people typically don't describe their lives with excessive enthusiasm. Indeed, there doesn't seem to be a relationship between enthusiasm and happiness. Rather, those who describe themselves as truly happy speak of *continuing satisfaction* rather than their periodic successes or failures. They enjoy their work, their spouses, and their families. They actively engage in personal, familial, or business plans and pursuits. They rarely complain about their parents or their bosses, even though they face as much difficulty as others from time to time.

What's different? Happy people make conscious decisions to avoid any *stoppers* to their happiness.

As they pursue what they want in life, they're not passive in their responses to problems and opportunities. Sure, they might worry about their careers, marriages, and children's education. But they lack resentment when things go badly and never feel envy when good fortune shines on others. They believe unfairness is part of life. They're thoughtful about their actions and have multiple goals they're striving for. They believe that facing difficult choices is inevitable because, in the real world, time and resources are always in short supply.

The complexity of pursuing multiple ends leads to having to choose—

- What to do right now.
- What priorities to set.
- How to sequence and integrate the ends.

Within this process, making good choices is critical for happiness. So is figuring out how to balance competing parts, which are challenges both Bob and Brenda face. The good news is, Aristotle's Theory of the Mean (discussed in Chapter 4) will guide the way!

The Lack of Precision

By most accounts, Aristotle is one of the wisest people who ever lived. He reminds those who'll listen to apply rational thought to make the right decisions in life, thus increasing our chances for happiness.

Certainly, if you find and follow a good recipe for being happy, you've taken a major step toward finding happiness itself. Having a good recipe for a cake doesn't mean it's the best recipe that exists. Still, having *any* reasonable recipe is better than having no recipe at all.

Notwithstanding his wisdom, Aristotle acknowledged the limits on how precise people can expect to be when measuring happiness. And this lack of precision is only the beginning. He said, "We must be content, then, in speaking of such subjects and with such premises to indicate the truth roughly and in outline, and in speaking about such things which are only for the most part true in and with premises of the same kind to reach conclusions that are no better" (*NE* 1094b19). Agreed, many of the ingredients people consider necessary for happiness are difficult to define and measure.

For instance, even if you believe that a certain level of good health is necessary for happiness, how can you say exactly what "good health" is? Plus, it's difficult to say how much good health is enough. If someone were slightly less healthy than optimum, how much more health would be required for happiness? What factors would make up the difference?

What happens when you apply the same questions to wealth, friendship, honor, fame, or other things people commonly say they need to achieve happiness? These questions simply can't be answered precisely.

Still, don't let the problem of precision deter you from looking for reliable systems that can optimize your chances for a happy life.

Chapter 1: Summary of Concepts

According to Aristotle, happiness is an activity or a state actualized by an activity. Doing the right thing at the right time is considered virtuous action and is likely to bring happiness.

Aristotle's view proposes that you need to *do* something to reach happiness. That means notwithstanding the nature of luck, one should take the matter of achieving happiness into one's own hands.

Aristotle differentiates between *intelligence* and *excellence* by noting that a truly intelligent person sees the right course of action but might not always follow it. By comparison, an excellent (or virtuous) person sees the right thing to do *and* takes the right action. He or she does the right thing, at the right time, *for the right person, and in the right way. This gives you reason to pause and reflect on how and why* you might fail to act even when you know the right thing to do.

Instead of overemphasizing one goal, such as success, it's better to focus on a multiplicity of ends.

Aristotle observes that when you allow your emotions to be in charge, your thinking isn't guided by reason. Therefore, to avoid a *stopper* to happiness, you need to control your emotions and use reasoning to conclude what's best. The problem arises when you know the right thing to do and don't act on it because of one kind of *stopper* or another. That tells you to be aware of your emotions and not act impulsively. When you know the right thing to do, then you must act in a timely and rational manner.

The definition of happiness is imprecise and its measurement impossible. Still, Aristotle says that (1) everyone pursues happiness, and (2) the kind of happiness everyone pursues is identical.

Points to Think About

1. Once you have reached happiness, nothing can make you happier.

2. Think of your rational mind as the *general* and your emotions as the *lieutenants.* The *general* is the boss and must control the *lieutenants.*
3. An intelligent person *knows* the right thing to do, while an excellent person *knows* and *does* the right thing, in the right way, at the right time, and for the right reason.
4. Actively doing the right thing constitutes *virtuous* action that's likely to result in happiness.
5. Conscious effort is required to confront and control *stoppers* to happiness.
6. Happiness refers to *continuing* life satisfaction but not necessarily being satisfied with all things at all times.

Dos and Don'ts

- *Do* use your intelligence as the tool for figuring out the correct action to take.
- *Do* control your emotions in order to do the right thing.
- *Don't* mistake shrewdness for intelligence.
- *Don't* neglect to act once you identify the correct action to take.

Take Action

1. Make a list of family, friends, coworkers, or community leaders who demonstrate shrewdness rather than intelligence as defined by Aristotle. What changes would you recommend for these people?
2. The concept of using your rational mind to control your behavior is reflected in adages such as these: "If you're angry, count to ten before you act" and "Look before you leap." Describe situations in which you have applied

Aristotle's definition of intelligence by modulating your emotions.

3. Describe areas in your life in which you know the right thing to do but don't do it. Then describe how you can use Aristotle's philosophy to do the right thing, in the right way, at the right time.

"It is absurd to make external circumstances responsible and not oneself."
—Aristotle (*NE* 1110b15)

Chapter 2: Responsibility

George is a quarterback for a football team in the National Football League. Harold, a young journalist conducting an interview for a local paper, asks George, "What's it like to be a quarterback in the NFL?"

For a moment, George seems taken aback. Finally, he asks Harold, "What do you mean, 'What is it like?'"

Harold responds, "So many people dream of being a quarterback. I would like to tell my readers what it's actually like to be a professional football player."

George closes his eyes and thoughtfully says, "I still don't know what you mean…."

Harold continues, "Well, for instance, does it hurt when the linemen hit you? Do you sometimes think you're silly for playing this game? How does it work in your head?"

George says, "First, yes, being hit hurts a lot; second, I have no regrets; and third, I don't think it's silly."

Harold goes on, "So does it mean anything to you that so many people are injured playing professional football? What impact does that have on your thinking?"

George's response provides Harold with a life lesson that applies to everyone. He says, "Listen, when you go into the National Football League, you don't think about the danger of an injury. You don't write home to your mother about ways all the big boys hit you and how it hurts. All of that is part of being a quarterback in the National Football League. You accept it or you do something else."

This life lesson reminds you to choose the game you play. Plan and dream your own dream—about going to school in medicine, engineering, law, or starting a business—whatever. Those who do provide examples of people who consciously chose their game.

Yet, many others feel they didn't make a choice at all. They dream of their "road not taken" (Frost, 1920) and in some way, feel cheated out of an ideal life based on a variety of different causes. For example, there are those who—

- married at an early age, have families, and describe themselves as "trapped."
- went into military service to escape choosing which road to follow.
- gave no thought about what road to follow and now feel directionless.
- say they were coerced by parents (or others) to follow one road or another.
- chose a career in a profession and now believe that choice is irreversible.

The common denominator? This group of people won't take responsibility for their "road"—the path they chose to walk—being the way it is today. Perhaps they didn't see their choices as being their personal responsibility. But they might change their viewpoint after answering these questions:

- Did anyone force them to choose or not choose their path?
- Do they think a different choice would have necessarily rendered a different result?
- Do they think their parents or other important adults forced them into choices?
- Would they admit that they, in the end, are responsible for what road was chosen?
- Do they suffer with regret today from thinking about "the road not taken"?

Contemplating Responsibility

In truth, few people are ever physically required to take the path they took. For those individuals who believe they just "fell into" whatever they're doing today, it's helpful to their progress to assume full responsibility for what's happened in their lives. For those who think they had no opportunity for a thoughtful choice at a young age, it's helpful to know that *some* young people grabbed opportunities to make thoughtful choices.

By accepting responsibility for yourself today, you know you still have the opportunity to choose and change. You're not required to choose in any particular way. Knowing that can free up all future decisions!

Of course, consequences come with every choice you make. As the NFL quarterback George says, "Yes, there is pain in playing this game." There is pain in all games, with each having its particular rules and risks. Evaluate all risks (including the possibility of bad luck) before you "take the field." And don't become a victim of bad luck; no one will listen anyway. In the same way George expresses, take responsibility for whatever happens to you.

It's particularly important to take responsibility when things go badly. George knows that just as any attempted pass can be incomplete, any play can result in an injury. And just as every game has a winner and a loser, the possibility of failure is an accepted part of playing the game.

What happens when you avoid responsibility for a problem you've caused? You lose credibility. In fact, you could lose credibility when you avoid responsibility for a problem you *conceivably* caused.

However, you can deal with taking responsibility more easily when you consider these points Aristotle made:

- We need to *do* something for happiness.
- We can't allow inevitable challenges to send us into a downspin (NE 1100b5).

Don't believe that any other life plan you might have chosen would be ideal. Each one brings its own set of problems for which you must take responsibility. For instance, perhaps you think, "I wish I'd become an architect instead of a lawyer because my problems would be fewer." Not true. And any resentment you might feel as a result makes no sense. Each life brings its own quota of problems, some of which you have caused.

Accepting Responsibility

Aristotle said, "Some are thought to have fairly good opinions, but by reason of vice choose what they should not" (*NE* 1112a10).

Any system of ethics considers the question of moral responsibility—(1) people have to make choices, moral and otherwise, and (2) they're responsible for the voluntary choices they make. An involuntary choice would be a man holding a gun to your head to force you to do something against your will. In that case, you may not be responsible for the choice you make. Aristotle makes it clear that, if people make voluntary and rational choices, they're responsible for them being the *correct* choices. Some people, Aristotle pointed out, know what to do but make bad choices (*NE* 1112a).

Accepting your responsibility helps you focus on creating solutions to whatever problems you face. Presumably, the stronger your focus, the better your chances of doing the right thing in the right way. And when you do the right thing in the right way, you enhance your chances for happiness. You'll avoid this *stopper* to happiness by accepting as much responsibility as you can for problems that come your way.

Remember, Aristotle says you need to do something for happiness. And anytime you do something, accept the inherent risks in whatever you've chosen to do.

The Role Played by Luck

Aristotle wasn't naïve about the question of good and bad luck, believing that happiness can disappear with the onset of very bad luck. In addition, he said, "There are some things, the lack of which takes away from happiness. Such things involve good birth, good children, and beauty." He added, "The man who is very ugly in appearance or ill-born or solitary and childless is not very likely to be happy" (*NE* 1099b4).

Common sense supports the notion that luck plays a part in your chances for happiness. Yet, everyone risks experiencing bad luck. From the moment of your birth, you're subject to the whims of circumstance. Some people are born into dysfunctional families; others are born into poverty; still others are killed or injured in disasters (e.g., car or plane crashes, floods, tornadoes, hurricanes, etc.). Innocent people get murdered; loved ones die. When you're a victim of bad luck, you might find it difficult to attain or maintain your happiness.

Also making it difficult to achieve or maintain happiness is moral luck, which is discussed in several philosophical circles. In

Moral Questions (Nagel, 1979) and *Moral Luck* (Williams, 1983), the authors describe unfortunate situations that many face, circumstances about which they feel morally responsible regardless of the fact that they had no control. For example:

> *A grandfather, Tom, is taking his four-year-old grandchild, Jordon, to the movies. Tom drives responsibly and at a legal speed in a car he knows is in good condition. He has it serviced regularly and recently had the brakes checked. He has put Jordon in an appropriate car seat wearing a child's seat belt.*
>
> *Suddenly, a drunk driver hits Tom's car. Jordon dies. After an investigation, Tom is judged to have had no responsibility for causing this tragedy. In fact, every witness and detective declares that Tom was driving as safely as possible.*
>
> *Regardless, the world changes for Tom. After all, at the time of the accident, Tom was in charge of Jordon's safety. He feels morally responsible even though he did nothing wrong. His daughter and people in the world at large (although they'd deny it) seem to regard him as if he were morally responsible for his grandchild's death.*

This story of moral luck is unpredictable and uncontrollable. Moreover, it manifests itself much more often than people realize.

Notwithstanding the unpredictable and uncontrolled nature of luck, it's important to take the matter of achieving happiness into your own hands to the greatest extent possible. In doing so, distinguish between the kind of bad luck confronted due to, say, a disability at birth and the kind that includes moral luck. In the first case, although you don't have the power to avoid a birth disability, you can make a rational plan for happiness and implement it within the constraints of your disability. In the second case, you know about the possibility of bad luck and can rationally include it in your expectations. So when it comes your way, you're better prepared to respond in the best way possible and minimize the damage.

Shared Responsibility

As a young man, Ryan worked on a construction crew. He and another worker were remodeling a school and had to carry the old slate blackboards down three flights of winding stairs to the playground. Ryan learned the hard way the heaviness of that slate.

He was only sixteen, but his work partner, John, was in his forties. A laborer all his life, John was as strong as a man can be. To do this task, he took the front of the eight-foot-long slate slabs going down the steps—the heavier part of the load.

Ryan recalls how, on one particular trip down the steps, he warned John repeatedly to be careful—"watch the steps, look out for the turn," and so on. When they finally got down to the playground, Ryan cautioned John again as they set the slate on the ground. John hadn't said anything while moving the slates, but after the last one was laid on the ground, he turned to Ryan and said quietly and firmly, "Young man, if you watch me and I watch you, somebody will get hurt. If you watch yourself and I watch myself, then we'll be all right."

John was correct to chastise the inexperienced young man. John was perfectly capable of taking care of himself, and Ryan's concern was excessive and even disrespectful. Perhaps Ryan was masking concern about his own ability to carry his side of the blackboard.

In another situation, Gary recalls when his friend Linda was caught up in the midst of a business crisis.

Linda's construction company was out of money and midway through a number of previously contracted construction projects. To recover successfully and deal with this state of affairs, it desperately needed an infusion of $500,000.

As the company sank deeper into difficulty, the tension between Linda and her partners escalated. The group scheduled a meeting to develop an action plan. If the company didn't get these construction jobs completed on time, the result would be unfinished and unmarketable structures confiscated by the banks. If this happened, the company would suffer a devastating loss—probably enough of a loss to put the company out of business. That would mean the partners losing much of their net worth as a result of being unable to recover this large investment. Their choice? Either to abandon the projects and accept a total loss, or find and inject $500,000 of new money to save the projects. However, no one in the group could put up that much money individually.

Shortly after Linda walked into the meeting to confront her troubled partners, she announced with certainty she was completely, unambiguously responsible for this financial mess. She continued by saying, "No need to point fingers or debate who is responsible for this problem. I'm the responsible partner. However, that doesn't matter right now. For the benefit of all of us, we need to fix the problem if we want to survive.

"I have a total of $150,000 in my personal accounts. I'm making it all available right now to restart work on the completion of the jobs. By offering this money, I'm taking responsibility for the debacle and, at the same time, asking you to join with me to solve the problem. We need to work together to gather the money to finish the jobs—for the benefit of every one of us." One by one, the partners offered their own cash on

hand and were able to finance the completion of the jobs—and an eventual renewal of the company.

In this situation, Linda admitted responsibility for the difficulty. Certainly, in her own defense, she could have pointed out the mistakes she thought her team members had made. It's difficult for one person to stand up and take all the heat. Yet when Linda considered her leadership position and knew her own share of responsibility, she decided to simplify matters by assuming *all* responsibility. If Linda had instead allowed a debate about who was responsible, the meeting would likely have unraveled in mutual accusations, making it extremely difficult to focus on the problem of raising the money. Her actions allowed the group to deal with the problem at hand.

Most people want to protect themselves by not taking more responsibility than necessary. Indeed, if confronted, Linda's colleagues might have admitted their own mistakes and thus lessened the burden on Linda. But her feelings weren't at stake—and she knew it. Most important was having the group focus on the "fix." As Aristotle said, our character is determined by choosing the right thing to do, not by our opinions (*NE* 112a7).

Accepting Responsibility: An *Excellent* Person in Action

Often people deny responsibility for problems they've helped to create. Even when they know that accepting responsibility is the right and wise thing to do, they often deny their own culpability. They don't stand up and admit responsibility because they're afraid of the consequences to them.

So rather than assessing their own actions in search of possible wrongdoings, people look outward and accuse others. Aristotle says that an *excellent* person judges each thing correctly and sees what is true in each case (*NE* 1113a30). For this reason, Aristotle would judge Linda to be an excellent person for accepting both the reality of the company's circumstances and the politics of the situation. She had judged her partners correctly, putting aside wishful thinking, using the virtuous mean described in Chapter 4. She did neither too much nor too little.

A person lacking excellence would either—

- Not understand the existence or depth of the problem, or
- Be unable to accept responsibility.

Linda was neither fearful nor overconfident; rather, she exposed herself to the criticism that would come from accepting responsibility. Using her rational mind, she didn't allow her emotions to drive her behavior.

Happy people typically arrange all the important "bricks" of their life in a way that builds an excellent brick "wall." The bigger the stakes, the more important it becomes to use your analysis and logical decision-making skills. According to Aristotle, when emotions are too strong, thinking is not guided by reason (*NE* 1102b15). Thus, the better your reason controls your emotions, the better decisions you make. Aristotle said, "It's not easy, but an excellent person will do the right thing in all circumstances. For these reasons, such a person is rare" (*NE* 1140a25).

In this example, Linda proved to be both an *intelligent* person—in that she knew the right thing to do at the right time—and an *excellent* person—in that she took the right action. Reflecting rational, solution-based thinking, she immediately claimed responsibility and helped her colleagues focus on what mattered. In Linda's case, the critical act in turning the company around was the power she gained from assuming (rather than denying) responsibility for its problems. She told the truth about herself and the mistakes she made. If Linda had failed to be truthful, how different the outcome would have been!

On Lies and Truth Telling

"The happy man will be happy throughout his life; for always, or by preference to everything else, he will be engaged in virtuous action" (*NE* 1100b18).

Ethan, a brilliant young salesperson in a brokerage company, is embezzling from its client investment accounts. He conceals the crime with fictitious reports showing exaggerated positive investment results. These overstated positive results lead his clients to have increasingly higher levels of confidence in his recommendations. As a result, Ethan's business is growing, he's gaining more confidence, and he's earning more esteem from both his clients and his colleagues. Ethan travels in a private jet and lives an extravagant life—all the benefits you'd expect of a very rich, intelligent man.

But his "success" is short-lived. His fraud is discovered when a client calls to redeem his portfolio and can't get the funds. Shocked, people are asking one another why Ethan would have done such a thing. They wonder whether he's nearly as happy as he seems and if his "charmed life" could ever be worth the worry he must have suffered. In the end, Ethan confesses to his crime and receives a sentence of twenty years in prison.

Phyllis, a business colleague, offered this opinion about Ethan's situation: "Ethan had no thought that anything mattered about the way he was getting the money. Everything was about the payoff he got from the outside world. From Ethan's perspective, if he hadn't been caught, he would have had the good life—money, status, power. No one would have known or cared whether he achieved it dishonestly. In the end, the only thing relevant about what happened to Ethan is that he was caught and sent to prison."

Phyllis's comments might lead you to ask, "How could Ethan's lying not be a *stopper* to happiness?" After all, happiness according to Aristotle depends on doing the right thing for the right person. People who lie destroy the ability to reason and to decide the correct action to take. Yet Ethan does the *opposite* of the right thing. For him, lies became a barrier or a *stopper* to his happiness.

> *Some time ago when Gary was teaching a seminar, he talked about the need for telling the truth as a prerequisite to finding happiness. An attendee named Karen objected to this, pointing out that her late husband, Norman, lied often and without compunction. A successful executive, he enjoyed the esteem of both his colleagues and many friends at the country club where he and Karen were members. Norman would constantly tell her about people he had lied to so he could "make a buck." In response, Gary suggested that Norman was probably anxious and unhappy about all the lies he told. "On the contrary," replied Karen, "Norman has always been a very happy person—sleeping soundly and showing no remorse for his lying." To add insult to injury, she told Gary to "get out of your ivory tower" and learn the way the world actually works. That is, people lie all the time to get what they want—in business and in personal relationships.*

Notwithstanding Karen's view, lying stops happiness. Who could rationally think that a life built on lies could be a good life? Doing the right thing, for the right person, at the right time is critical for happiness. Attempts by Ethan and Norman to justify lying during the conduct of business weren't rational. In fact, lying in business destroys sound reasoning and lasting relationships.

You can't retain quality clients without being completely truthful. Actions that are destructive to sound reasoning create a *stopper* to happiness and can ruin business. Over time, retaining good customers has infinitely more value than any short- or medium-term gain from a group of transactions. Long-term winners tell the truth and accumulate credibility. For this reason, repeat business and prosperity follow.

Imagine what goes through the mind of a successful person who has lied his way to success and continues lying to maintain it. First, he likely holds on to the fear of discovery by those he has wronged. Second, if his lies cross legal boundaries, he lives in fear of prosecution despite how confident or safe from detection he feels. If he thinks rationally at all, he is building *stoppers* to his happiness with every lie he tells.

This is true even when you simply lie to exaggerate your own status or accomplishments. It's also true of people who live beyond their means and/or try to impress others. What feelings are associated with constantly pursuing the respect of others by *misrepresenting* yourself?

In contrast, happy people don't wish to be seen as anything other than who they are. When what you present to the world is truthful, you'll experience continuing satisfaction mixed with the possibility of happiness.

When It's Right to Lie

Aristotle said, "The accounts we demand must be in accordance with the subject matter" (*NE* 1104a4). That means thinking about a particular situation before deciding what to do—which might lead to exceptions to the rule "don't lie."

> *Suppose you're on a street corner minding your own business when you see a terribly frightened woman run past you screaming, "Help me! Help me! He's going to kill me!" Then she zips into an alleyway and vanishes. A few moments later,*

from the same direction the woman came, you see a man with a gun coming toward you. As the man races by, he asks, "Did you see a woman running down the street?"

In this circumstance, it's right to lie to the gunman about where the woman went. But don't confuse this with trivial or "white" lies. When you say a white lie, skirt the truth, or tell a lie of omission, you seek to avoid a negative consequence like hurting someone's feelings or fearing someone's harsh reaction. But saving face or avoiding conflict is not justification for compromising the truth. Doing the right thing at the right time requires honesty and respecting another's need for truthfulness. As Aristotle said, "Intelligence requires evaluation about us and the circumstances" (*NE* 1107a4).

Chapter 2: Summary of Concepts

Finding happiness requires doing the right thing—and the first "right thing" is to assume responsibility for your actions. Accept the inevitable that life will present problems—some you can't control, others you cause, and still others you can make worse. In all these cases, actively seek and accept your responsibility in what happens.

Acknowledge the possibility of failure at the start of each endeavor, thus making it easier to accept responsibility for things that go wrong. When you stop being concerned with who's responsible for a failed endeavor, you can focus on overcoming obstacles. In the end, you'll increase the possibility of a good result by taking responsibility for a failure before, during, and after any endeavor. In any case, when you accept responsibility and avoid lying, you minimize the *stoppers* that reduce your chances for happiness.

Aristotle expressed awareness of the huge effect bad luck can have on one's chances for happiness. If you're born in the wrong place to the wrong people or with some major physical defect, you might believe happiness is hard or impossible to reach. Again, not true. From time to time, happiness can disappear with very bad luck. Most of the time, however, it's within your reach if you act in the right way.

Points to Think About

1. The more responsibility you take for things gone wrong, the better off you are.
2. When you deny responsibility for a problem, you often make the problem worse.
3. You actively choose to play the game you play while understanding that each game has its own particular pain.
4. Telling even small lies is a *stopper* to happiness.
5. It is no more acceptable to tell lies in one's business dealings than in one's personal life.
6. Overstating your accomplishments—both implicitly and explicitly—is a form of lying.
7. Exceptions to the "no lying" rule exist, but primarily when someone's safety is in question.

Dos and Don'ts

- *Do* take responsibility for your failures and mistakes without being overly concerned with other people's responsibility.
- *Do* establish conditions that encourage honesty at home and work.
- *Don't* assume you can attain happiness without experiencing some mistakes or failures.
- *Don't* justify yourself or accept the justifications of others about telling a lie.

Take Action

1. Describe situations during which you failed to take appropriate and immediate responsibility. Given another chance, how would you handle it differently?
2. Think about people who seem to be happy and describe how they accept responsibility.
3. Consider people you know personally or professionally who overstate their accomplishments. How do those exaggerations affect your respect for them?

"... and there are some things the lack of which
takes the luster from happiness."
—Aristotle (*NE* 1099b3)

Chapter 3: Fame and Fortune

Tiger Woods became famous for being the best golfer in the world, earning hundreds of millions of dollars in prize money and endorsements. Until recently, he was revered as one of the most successful and admired athletes in the world. Suddenly, his life fell apart as a result of personal choices, and today, he struggles to find his way out of his personal and professional difficulties.

People of all ages know the story of Marilyn Monroe—the world's most famous movie star and considered one of the richest, most beautiful women of her era. She was at the height of her success when she committed suicide. While no one will ever know why for certain, she was reportedly an unhappy person who felt dissatisfied with her life. Marilyn Monroe's fame and fortune didn't bring her happiness.

Every generation provides examples of the "disconnect" between having success and achieving happiness. Woods is a star athlete of the twenty-first century, while Monroe starred in the 1950s. Both have become icons of the rich, successful, powerful—and unhappy.

A person can appear to "have it all" and still feel unhappy. The stars on the red carpet *look* so happy, it's hard to believe they may not *be* happy. And the nature of competition involves winners and losers. It's a mistake, however, to attribute unrelated positive characteristics (e.g., good judgment) to the stars. Let's look more closely at the relationship between fame/fortune and happiness.

Three Categories of Life Requirements

Aristotle said that all the good things in life can be divided into these three classes:

- *Necessities of life:* all the things people naturally pursue including good health, exercise, sexuality, and physical needs. Aristotle pointed out that all animals naturally seek some or all of these kinds of ends, too.
- *External goods:* all the material possessions needed to create a sense of family and financial well-being. Unfortunately, people commonly overemphasize the importance of financial success.
- *Goods of the soul:* the important thing to note about goods of the soul is that "goods of the body and external goods are desirable and necessary, but goods of the soul are unique to human beings and are the most important ends for happiness" (*NE* 1098a13).

Only human beings can pursue *goods of the soul* such as generosity, courage, and ethical behavior because this quest requires the rationality of the human mind. The challenge is in making the best decisions to attain the best result.

When you see people who are rich and famous, you're actually seeing the big winners of the *external goods.* Some have good health as well as financial well-being. You might assume that if they have health and plenty of money, they will naturally be happy. But you can't know if these rich and healthy people have *goods of the soul.* According to Aristotle, a person who has health and a lot of money but lacks *goods of the soul* is missing the most important attribute a human being can possess—happiness.

How Much Is Enough?

Happiness, as described by Aristotle, means a permanent satisfaction with life. To have this satisfaction, Aristotle said it requires a minimum amount of money or what money can buy (*NE* 1099b5). But you need to answer these three important questions:

1. What do you believe is the minimum amount of money needed to have a chance for happiness?
2. Suppose you have that minimum amount of money needed for happiness. Does additional money add to your happiness?
3. Why do rich yet unhappy people believe that having more money will help them move toward happiness?

As a metaphor for minimum financial need, compare a person who owns a Volkswagen with someone who owns a Rolls Royce. To get around town, the Volkswagen meets minimum transportation requirements—therefore, the owner of the Volkswagen can be positioned for happiness just as well as the person who owns the Rolls Royce. Because both have solved their need for transportation, adding more cars won't add anything to each individual's happiness.

Still, it seems that both owners should have a better chance for happiness than the person who doesn't own a car at all. Yet you'll find this isn't necessarily true when you ask, "Is the person's life really impaired by the absence of an automobile?"

Unnecessary excess might also be the difference between owning a mansion compared with owning a tract house. Again, once the minimum space needed to be happy is satisfied, more square footage doesn't add to one's happiness. For example, if a thousand square foot in a house or apartment has been tagged as "the minimum" needed for happiness, an extra one thousand square feet would be meaningless for this purpose. However, that minimum changes if ten rather than two people live in those thousand square feet.

In your quest for happiness, one of the keys to making good decisions is evaluating the minimum needed for happiness based on particular circumstances. This means every person meeting the minimum can achieve happiness in the same way. For example, if individual A says he's happy and individual B says she's happy, it means they experience the same ongoing satisfaction with life. It makes no difference, therefore, if happy person A has a bigger house than happy person B; both have enough for "happiness purposes." Indeed, once you get to the "happiness finish line," the race to happiness ends.

However, if you're confused about the relationship between money and happiness, it can lead to the pursuit of money as the most dominant objective—something that can create a *stopper* to your chances for happiness. The *stopper* is profound disappointment—the kind that comes to Rolls Royce owners when they realize the happiness they expected from being financially successful hasn't resulted in happiness. This doesn't suggest that having excess net worth leads to *unhappiness*. Rather, it emphasizes that any excess means nothing as far as happiness goes.

Measuring Success and Happiness

While you can measure if someone is *successful*, you can't measure if someone is happy. To evaluate happiness, the best you can do is to ask a person and make a judgment based on the answers you get. And because it can't be reliably measured, happiness can't be compared from one person to the next.

Yet you *can* compare one's success to another's. Among those who aspire to high office, for example, a person elected to US Congress and another elected as president are both considered successful politicians. After all, they've both been elected to high office. Yet because the presidency is a higher position than a Congressional representative, the president elect is deemed a more successful politician than the one elected to Congress.

In the same way, you might identify the most successful businessman as the one who's made the most money. Yet you can't know through observing their level of success if the most successful politician or the most successful businessperson is happy. Here's an example.

At the beginning of the twenty-first century, Vice President Al Gore lost a highly contested presidential election to Texas Governor George W. Bush. President Bush went on to experience two challenging terms in his presidency, facing terrorism and two wars as well as an historic economic crisis. Gore, on the other hand, left formal politics, pursued a life in environmental activism, and went on to win the Nobel Peace Prize. Later still, Gore and his wife got divorced and President Bush, his term of office over, moved back to Texas. At the end of the day, we have no idea whether Gore is happy and Bush is not, or vice versa. Happiness, unlike success, cannot be measured.

Measuring Power and Happiness

People pursue power in much the same way they pursue fame and fortune. Power, however, doesn't bring happiness any more than fame or fortune does.

Larry, a lawyer in his sixties, had built and managed a large law firm. He made a lot of money, was honored by the national legal community, and had a great deal of power over the lives of others. What he did or did not do affected the careers and lives of dozens of people with whom he worked. Consequently, almost without exception, people showed him honor and respect, at least at the surface level. Usually they deferred to his opinions and did as he wished.

Much later, Larry learned that people felt intimidated and controlled by the power he held over them. When he retired, he was aghast to see how his use of power had influenced the honesty of his relationships. He had no way to assess whether his ability to influence others resulted from his position of authority, his personality, his intellect, or all of them.

The most troubling post-retirement experience for Larry was the huge difference in the way people responded to him. When he held authority positions, people eagerly listened to his opinions on almost any subject. Now that he's retired, his former colleagues show little interest in his opinion. Worse yet, people who had disliked him for years (he had no idea) made their feelings clear to him. Simply stated, they no longer feared him.

Larry had assumed that the relationships he'd developed throughout his career would remain the same after his retirement, but he'd misunderstood many of them. He didn't comprehend his power over the people he worked with. Certainly, before he retired, he'd met people who mildly (not contentiously) disagreed with him. However, no one had resisted his ideas because people couldn't express strong opposing opinions without taking a risk with him. Larry hadn't known that the power of his position—not the power of his ideas—caused them to respond to him that way. Yet without having any friendships to carry into his retirement years, Larry said the honors he'd received during his career didn't mean much.

How much power over others could a golfer, an actress, or a lawyer possess? Power emanates from their ability to help others and is exerted through money, jobs, contacts, and a myriad of other ways. People in authority positions like Larry misunderstand how their power can potentially confuse others when it comes to personal relationships. The old saying—originally written by Lord Action (1834–1902) in an 1887 letter to Bishop Creighton—holds that "power corrupts, and absolute power corrupts absolutely." Ironically, this aspect of the human condition can potentially be a *stopper* to the powerful person.

If you (1) have power over others and believe that your power is permanent or "the way things should be," or (2) believe those you hold authority or power over are telling you what they really think, you're facing a *stopper* over the long run. For their own safety, people you have power over appear to respect you. But sooner or later, the truth unfolds. When it does, as it did for Larry, the resulting disappointment is the *stopper.*

This doesn't imply that people will simply lie to get what they want. Rather, it reflects a need to illuminate and understand the limit of your own power over others. Actually, it raises the question of whether such power has any true meaning. It's what Aristotle describes as thinking about what is *really* good and what promotes living well (*NE* 1140b20).

Thoughts about Honor

Society has the ability to give to and take away from an individual any particular honor. But those people honored may or may not be honorable themselves. Aristotle pointed out that people of character don't *pursue* honors. However, they will *accept* an honor if (1) it's not for trivial actions, (2) it's truly earned, and (3) the action that brought the honor was the right thing to do for the right reason (*NE* 1123b25).

That's why you might not be aware of countless honorable acts that occur. Unknown honorable acts can't be acknowledged because people of character who do them don't pursue honors. Rather, they perform these acts anonymously much of the time. As Aristotle said, the pursuit of *being honored,* rather than being *honorable,* has the potential of being a *stopper* to your happiness.

Remember, being virtuous or honorable involves doing the right thing, for the right person, at the right time, and for the right reason—thus opening the door to happiness. If you receive an honor for significant achievement, then know that it's something virtuous people can accept. Accepting honors for something trivial or something you don't deserve usually is a *stopper.*

Winning and Losing

The possibility of winning or losing remains constant in today's world. People struggle to be successful, to win at the games they play, and to succeed in their businesses. During the course of pursuing victories, some engage in unethical and/or illegal activities to "win." They wrongly conclude nothing about this behavior reduces the chance for happiness. It seems that they don't think about the idea that wrong-headed behavior can be a *stopper* to happiness. Apparently, to them, it is only a matter of whether they're caught.

Too Much Tunnel Vision

People like Bob, the retired developer (described in Chapter 1), as well as Tiger Woods and Marilyn Monroe (discussed earlier in this chapter) make crucial mistakes when they pursue fame or fortune to the extent that they ignore everything else. Focusing on one end (goal) may create a *stopper* to your happiness, plus it's not what an *intelligent* person does. Give up the hope *right now* that any one achievement (like being rich or famous) will necessarily bring you happiness.

In today's frenzied 24/7 world, when you're pursuing a number of goals, it's easy to feel overwhelmed and out of balance. The next chapter describes Aristotle's views about avoiding this problem and provides us with a tool in his Theory of the Mean.

Chapter 3: Summary of Concepts

Much evidence shows that achieving fame, acquiring fortune, and/or receiving honors don't necessarily bring happiness. Yet the evidence gets ignored by continuing to believe that fame and fortune can "give birth" to a happy life. It can be difficult to grasp the idea that wealthy or famous people aren't necessarily happy. Worse yet, some people seem to think that the *only* thing that matters is success. As a result, these people face an obstacle or *stopper* to their own happiness.

Unquestionably, fame and fortune can seduce with excitement, but examples abound of people who failed to find happiness despite their achievements. In some cases, the greater the success, the less happiness successful people enjoy. The trick? Remember, its not one single end—honors, fame, or fortune—that ensures happiness. In fact, having only one goal can lead to living an unbalanced (and often empty) life.

Although you can divide all aspects of your life into three categories, being able to focus on *goods of the soul* is a gift enjoyed only by humans. Aristotle's lessons place life's emphasis on *goods of the soul*, such as kindness and generosity.

The possibility of winning or losing constantly plagues us. It's important to avoid taking shortcuts in order to win—and the same goes for telling the truth, given that lying destroys the capacity for wise decision-making.

Points to Think About

1. People with a lot of money or celebrity have no better chance of attaining happiness than you do.
2. Overemphasizing the accumulation of material goods or becoming famous is a *stopper.*

3. Confusing a moment of pleasure with permanent satisfaction with life is a *stopper.*
4. People can be financially successful without being happy; people can be happy without being "successful."
5. It doesn't take a lot of money to be happy.

Dos and Don'ts

- *Do* ponder your life objectives and focus on *goods of the soul.*
- *Do* accept honors and awards that you earn for achievements that are not trivial.
- *Don't* focus too much on acquiring external goods.
- *Don't* encourage others to pursue honors and awards as a path to happiness.
- *Don't* think that people you've had power over necessarily respect you.

Take Action

1. Envision yourself as a movie star, athlete, or other celebrity. In what ways would that status make it harder for you to emphasize *goods of the soul*?
2. Describe successes and awards you've pursued in any important area of your life. Whether you have won or lost, succeeded or failed, describe the lessons you've learned. Include your thoughts about how the experience affected (or didn't affect) your happiness.
3. Answer this question for yourself: "What's wrong with accepting honors for trivial accomplishments?"

"But to feel [passion] and take [action] at the right time, with reference to the right objects, toward the right people, with the right motive toward the right object, and in the right way … this is what is both intermediate and best, and this is characteristic of virtue."
—Aristotle (*NE* 1106b20)

Chapter 4: Balance

Joseph was one of the smartest people you could ever meet. Among his accomplishments, he earned a doctorate in biochemistry from a major technical university. Joseph brags that there were three Nobel Prize winners on his doctoral committee. That, he adds, is about the scariest thing that can happen to a student at this level.

Joseph could solve baffling mathematical and logical problems. Despite his brainpower, however, he experienced a number of personal and family difficulties that could potentially be permanent stoppers to his happiness.

First, Joseph had distanced himself from his parents when they objected to his first marriage. Some time later, he divorced his first wife and became estranged from his two children. He remarried years later but remained distant from the children of his second wife. Everyone in his personal life thought he wasn't concerned about anything beyond his professional life and viewed him as a brilliant thinker but a disconnected individual. This story, however, has a successful conclusion. Joseph was able to start a new life.

> *Joseph was involved in an accident in which he and his family were nearly killed. During his long and difficult hospitalization and rehabilitation, Joseph started to revaluate his life. He asked himself, "Did I go off track by pursuing all of the professional activities and projects I thought were important?" Looking back, he saw that he had not fully realized the importance of a balanced life. By his own admission, Joseph failed the most important people in his life; he didn't do the right thing, at the right time, for the right people.*
>
> *Once he understood he'd made poor choices, Joseph focused on reorganizing his life, placing emphasis on his family as well as his intellectual life. With this seemingly simple decision, he eventually made things right with all his children. Noticeable to all—and especially himself—Joseph has achieved a balanced, happy life.*

Joseph's problems resulted from not using his monumental abilities to make thoughtful choices about the people in his life. As a result, he had exposed himself to a *stopper* that jeopardized his chances for happiness. He solved his problem when he took action consistent with Aristotle's Theory of the Mean.

The Theory of the Mean

In Aristotle's thinking, it takes a multiplicity of ends to find happiness because no one thing (end) can make a person happy. The problem arises when one feels confused about priorities resulting from having multiple objectives.

As explained in Chapter 1, virtue is defined as "a praiseworthy state of character of mind and soul." The problem is, when we want to do the right (virtuous) thing, it's often difficult to identify the right thing to do in a particular circumstance. In Joseph's case, for instance, after he was injured, he decided to pay more attention to his family. This change required him to pay less attention to his professional life. The question then became what to "keep" and what to "give up"? For example, Joseph would question if he should limit his travel so he can be home more. If he limited his travel, though, he'd be afraid he could not maintain the trajectory of his career. On the other hand, if he continued to travel, he'd miss many of his children's activities.

Quite naturally, Joseph is confused about his priorities. This is where Aristotle's theory enters the equation. Aristotle's Theory of the Mean provides a method for wisely determining virtuous (excellent) actions needed for happiness in everyday life. His Mean Theory is a continuum for identifying the mean between *excess* and *deficiency.* An example Aristotle might give is high mindedness, which is the mean between extreme pride *(excess)* and false humility *(deficiency*). This is the kind of calculation Joseph needed to make.

In a similar way, you can use this Theory of the Mean to make virtuous (excellent) decisions and avoid *stoppers* to your own happiness.

Agreeing on where the mean between excess and deficiency lies is not the same as agreeing to compromise so you can reach a peaceful solution. A compromise example would be (1) Joe says let's meet on Monday, (2) Greg says let's meet on Wednesday, and (3) they compromise and agree to meet on Tuesday.

However, this compromise differs from the Theory of the Mean, which functions as a compass for the wisest course of action. Referring to Joe and Greg, their meeting could occur on any of the three days. But when you apply the Theory of the Mean, what happens? You focus on doing the right thing. You have found the mean; you've acted correctly. This requires applying reason to foresee the consequences of your actions and using that insight to manage and balance your life. That's how it differs from compromising.

When looking at obvious examples of an unbalanced life, excess and deficiency are easy to see. Examples might include substance abuse, morbid obesity, or excessive gambling. Once you find the mean, acting on it would seem even easier. However, people can have difficulty (1) finding the mean and (2) acting on it—even when acting in accordance with a mean is important to their immediate situation.

What happens when people don't find the mean and make bad choices? Inevitably, it leads to experiencing a lack of balance that, in turn, acts as a *stopper* to their happiness.

Getting Off Track

Bart finally made partner at a large accounting firm. Because he works sixteen hours a day, he has little time to spend with his wife and children. Financially speaking, the family is doing well. They live in a large house in one of the most prestigious areas of Los Angeles. He and his wife drive luxurious cars. Their kids go to some of the best private schools in the area. On paper, life couldn't be better.

Bart knows he has much to be grateful for, yet he expresses sadness about his life. Both he and his wife dreamed of the material life they are leading. However, now that it's happening, it's not what he expected when he was going through business school and rising through the firm. He says he'd like to spend more time with his family, but if he cuts his hours, he will lose his chance for partnership bonuses that he needs to support their lifestyle. In the process, he doesn't know if he's making some hard-to-identify mistakes. He often thinks to himself that, regardless of outward appearances, his life is out of balance.

How to Find the Mean

Like Joseph the biochemist, Bart encounters a *stopper* because he isn't sufficiently thoughtful about the time conflict between all his ends. From Bart's perspective, he's too single-minded about success at the accountancy firm. Yet plenty of ways exist to both enjoy success and stay in balance. All require thought and determination.

To achieve both success and balance, focus your thinking on—

- The combination of goals you should pursue.
- The priority or emphasis to place on each goal.
- The *stoppers* to happiness you'll experience if you make bad choices.
- Not limiting yourself to one dominant goal, which can be a *stopper* to enjoying a balanced, happy life.

Living on the Mean

Bill makes a decent living owning a profitable computer software company, and he and his wife have three grown children. However, he's not completely satisfied with his income level, and it seems he's always dealing with problems in the business or within the family.

Although Bill doesn't expect his life to be perfect, he does admit it can be frustrating because of the financial, marital, educational, and other difficulties that pop up. At the end of the day, though, he accepts these situations as natural and generally feels okay with this imperfect state. Going forward, he's committed to thinking about all of his goals and objectives.

Bill understands that happiness comes from a life that balances several goals or, as Aristotle puts it, a multiplicity of ends. This accounts for his remaining in a state of *general* satisfaction. The accountant Bart, on the other hand, remains the victim of his own insufficiently thought-out ambition. Bart expected his financial success and professional stature to answer the happiness question. But he lost balance in his life because he didn't choose the right things to do. Joseph had also made unwise decisions, neglecting his family, but he made changes and his life became more balanced as he got older.

The Theory of the Mean is a tool to use in a multitude of life's circumstances. Joseph's story is similar to Bart's because they're both caught in the pursuit of a single end or goal. As a result, they forget about the other things needed for happiness. Neither Bart nor Joseph foresaw the negative consequences of their single-minded professional pursuit. Although Joseph eventually corrected his imbalance, both men experienced unhappiness because they were unaware of the need for a multiplicity of ends or variety of goals. Not paying enough attention to the negative consequence of pursuing goals seems to be a commonplace *stopper.*

Remember, the Theory of the Mean isn't meant to find compromise. Rather, when you seek the mean, you strive to identify the wisest course of action. Use the Theory of the Mean to help you go about your activities in the most virtuous way.

For instance, if you suspect a deficiency in the attention you provide to your family, or if you suspect your excessive family time is deterring you from personal or professional development, then question how you're applying reason. Look for the mean between excess and deficiency. Being thoughtful about your issues increases the possibility of living a life that's more balanced than ever.

Chapter 4: Summary of Concepts

Aristotle's Theory of the Mean provides a way to wisely determine appropriate and virtuous behavior. It becomes a tool to discern what actions are appropriate (virtuous) in the course of everyday life. It is, effectively, a continuum that measures virtuous action by finding the mean between deficiency and excess. Using this tool can help you avoid *stoppers* to your own happiness.

If you have multiple goals, you need to figure out how to balance competing parts of your life. Remember that, according to Aristotle, happiness requires constant work and thought—first in determining the mean and second in taking action to achieve your objectives.

Finding the mean between excess and deficiency isn't just agreeing to disagree and compromising for a peaceful solution. Rather, the mean functions as a compass directing you to the wisest course of action. When you use the mean as your guide, your actions will bring balance and harmony to your life.

The mean aims at the "balance point" between emotions and actions. That's why it's hard to be virtuous in all of your actions. In every case, you need to find the middle ground by (1) using your intelligence to accurately assess the rightness or wrongness of your actions, (2) applying that insight to manage and balance your life, and (3) increasing the number of your goals to achieve a multiplicity of ends.

Points to Think About

1. Wisdom, also known as moral virtue, is found at the midpoint between excess and deficiency. This is true for all our thoughts and actions.
2. The Theory of the Mean is Aristotle's tool to help determine the midpoint between too much and too little within everyday life.
3. If you find that your actions are not consistent with the mean, then you can quickly change.
4. There is no single accomplishment that ensures happiness. Happiness is comprised of a multiplicity of ends. It is the

actions one takes in pursuing these ends that provides the basis for a happy life.

5. Most of us have more issues than we can handle. Focus on what you are doing in the moment.

Dos and Don'ts

- *Do* try to find balance in all areas of your life. Look for the midpoint between too much and too little.
- *Do* avoid thinking that any particular thing you acquire or achieve will bring you happiness.
- *Do* understand that happiness is continuing *general* life satisfaction, not satisfaction with all things at all times.
- *Don't* be blinded to the negative effects that result from emphasizing success.
- *Don't* think you can achieve happiness without a great deal of thought as to how to find the mean and how to act in accordance with the mean.
- *Don't* confuse finding the mean between extremes with finding a compromise.

Take Action

1. Describe how Joseph acts and what makes him so happy. List actions you can take to achieve what Joseph has achieved.
2. Identify people who appear to be happy. Through conversation and observation, try to determine what they do to achieve happiness. List what you think they do to attain their feelings of satisfaction with their lives.
3. If you have one dominant goal, name it. Then describe how this pursuit helps or hinders your feelings of satisfaction or happiness. In what ways do you want to achieve more balance in your life?

"With regard to happiness … the same man identifies it with health when he is ill, with wealth when he is poor."
—Aristotle (*NE* 1095a23)

Chapter 5: Unrealistic Expectations

Gary gives a presentation on Aristotle's view about optimizing the chances for happiness by doing the right thing, for the right person, at the right time, and for the right reason. Jack, a successful real estate agent in the audience, says his experience is the opposite of what Gary espouses. He doesn't believe that doing the right thing optimizes one's chances for happiness.

"That's a bunch of baloney," Jack says. "You know, I try to help others all the time. I try to be generous with everyone I meet. I'm conscious of trying to do the right thing. But I'm constantly disappointed with people's responses to my efforts. For example, a couple of months ago, I went to a great deal of trouble to arrange for a friend to buy a new refrigerator at cost. I even arranged to have it delivered it without charge. I didn't expect payment, but I did expect appreciation for my efforts. What did my friend do in return? He bought a house from another real estate broker, even though he knows I could use the business. Obviously, my friend had no appreciation for what I did. This tells me there's no reason to believe that doing the 'right thing' helps at all.

"I have this kind of experience all the time. People just don't respond correctly to the good things I do for them."

Then Gary asks, "Jack, in a general way, do you feel like you're a person who tries to do the right thing for others?"

Jack says, "Yes. I try to help people all the time. Unfortunately, I think I'm not sufficiently appreciated or repaid for my efforts."

Gary asks, "In a general way, do you think you have a good life? From what I can see, you have a nice life. You seem prosperous. You have a nice family. It looks like a pretty good life."

Jack says, "I agree. I have a good life."

Gary went on, "Do you think there's any link between the way you do things and the way your life is? Not anything specific, such as when you helped your friend buy a refrigerator. I mean, in a general sense, do you think there's a relationship between the fact you try to do the right thing and the fact your life seems to be fine?"

Jack says, "I have to admit, there might be a connection. It seems my disappointment centers on expectations. Perhaps I should think about my motives for doing the right thing as well as managing my expectations. Perhaps my expectations aren't realistic."

You might ask, "What's the issue? Don't people usually have expectations similar to Jack's? Don't their motives for doing the right thing for others stem from an expectation that they'll get something back?"

The point is, if you expect reciprocation in order to do the right thing, you're not thinking in a manner consistent with Aristotle's advice about enhancing your chances for happiness. Remember, Aristotle said, "Doing the right thing, for the right reason, for the right person, is virtuous. And it's the virtuous thought and action that optimizes our chances for happiness." Aristotle did not say, "If you do the right thing for people, no matter what your motive, they will be appreciative, and you will be happy."

It makes no sense to think virtue consists of doing the right thing motivated by the wrong reason. Jack's self-serving motivation—

expecting reciprocation for his good deed—together with his unrealistic expectations established the *stopper.* When people think, "I deserve more," or "I'm entitled to more," or "I expect more," they lay the groundwork for a life of continuing disappointment.

Aristotle commented about expectations in a general way, saying people often think specific changes will bring about happiness. For instance, a poor man thinks wealth will bring about happiness. A wealthy man might think having a simpler, less financially driven lifestyle might bring happiness. When you make a change in your life (such as a move from the city to the country), your expectations can lead to disappointments—perhaps even a cascade of them. Feeling unhappy can easily result.

Even when you make a particularly profound change such as stopping addictive behavior, there's no concrete reason to believe happiness will result. When people are addicted to alcohol and stop drinking, for example, any expectation for happiness is unrealistic if it's based solely on the cessation of drinking. A newly honed ability to avoid drinking allows for the kind of virtuous actions required for happiness. To attain happiness, the virtuous actions need to start after the drinking stops.

A few common unrealistic expectations are: (1) people will always show appreciation for what you do, (2) specific success will bring you happiness, (3) your good reputation precedes you, and (4) your children, grandchildren, or other family members will understand what you've done for them.

Common Expectations

At great financial sacrifice, Noreen and Russell sent their children to top private universities. They expected, as many parents do, that graduating from a good school would give their children a greater chance for success and happiness. But they eventually came to understand that their expectations of a top university weren't realistic. Their children, now in their forties, are no more or less happy and successful than others their age who went to less sophisticated schools. It's not clear to Noreen and Russell that their children have any understanding of the financial sacrifices they'd made for them.

It's common for people to expect that a "good school" will lead their children to a successful and happy life. The same could be said about a "good marriage," or a "good job," or a "good bank account." Yet none of these good things on their own produces happiness. Decades later, after children endure life's disappointments, you see that prescripted systems for "the good life" don't necessarily produce the result you'd unrealistically expected.

The fact that you can't depend on any of these "good things" to produce happiness is no reason to despair. Yes, they're all encouraged and hoped for, but none provides the answer to happiness. Aristotle recommends certain *virtuous* actions for the purpose of bringing happiness. These actions would not include, for example, a student being accepted into Harvard. However, applying the discipline needed to earn excellent grades might be a good example of the kind of virtuous action Aristotle was talking about.

It becomes confusing because getting into Harvard seems like an important step toward a *successful* life. In all probability, it's good news. However, do eliminate unrealistic expectations that any particular successes will bring happiness. Remember, wealthy people often pledge to give up their riches when they're sick but demand the treasures back when their health has returned. These realities are all about expecting one particular thing to solve the problem.

Another kind of *stopper* can result from unrealistically expecting that winning in competition brings lasting satisfaction or even happiness. Aristotle's viewpoint does acknowledge the importance of competition. However, he qualifies his comments by pointing out the lesser importance of winning as opposed to the greater importance of competing. He says, "In the Olympic games it is not the most beautiful and the strongest that are crowned but those who compete" (*NE* 1099a6). He refers to the *action* of competing, not winning the competition, that matters when pursuing happiness. You may compete to be successful in both your personal and business lives; you might compete using the life games you play. Engaging in competition might be a part of what contributes to happiness. But to avoid a *stopper*, stay aware of the difference between (1) the kinds of actions necessary to win a competition, and (2) the kinds of actions necessary for happiness. The *stopper* develops when you believe that prevailing over others will bring happiness. A momentary triumph from winning at a game accomplishes no such thing.

Fun Doesn't Cut It

Will living a life of leisure and fun bring about happiness, as commonly believed? Aristotle doesn't deny the importance of entertainment and amusement. However, he said they're not the "endgame" (*NE* 1176b35). Rather, the endgame is a happy life composed of virtuous actions and, by necessity, serious actions that require exertion. Indeed, a life limited to fun and games comes with built-in *stoppers* to happiness. Such a life is not virtuous because it's—

- Entirely self-focused.
- Devoid of meaningful work that contributes to a sense of self-satisfaction when accomplished.
- Unlikely to include serious contemplation, thereby robbing you of the opportunity to experience positive aspects of the human condition more fully.

A happy life is not focused on leisure and fun; it requires serious activity. Some people express the idea that those who work when they are already wealthy have nothing but work in their lives. They presume these rich people have no hobbies or other interests to keep themselves busy. However, if they balance their work with leisure and fun, there's good reason for rich people to continue to work. They know they are exposed to unhappiness just as anyone else is. Such people can most likely foresee that, if they eliminate virtuous activity from their life, unhappiness is expected to follow. Indeed, they probably have more foresight than Bob, the developer described in Chapter 1 who found that golf didn't provide enough meaning in his life.

Every Day is a New Day

A common but unrealistic expectation is that your good reputation precedes you. As disappointing as it may be, it typically does not.

Cindy had risen to prominence nationally because of her spectacular sales. One year, she received honors for her commendable sales results. At the company sales meeting, the audience of seven hundred real estate agents and brokers buzzed with excitement to learn Cindy's secrets. One idea she shared related to unrealistic expectations.

Looking out over the crowd, she started, "You know, with all due respect, I think some of you might have an unrealistic view of what happens to me day by day. You might think, for instance, that because I'm so well known in the commercial real estate business, a new prospect's first response is, 'Wow. You're Cindy. I hear about you often. This is my lucky day. Will you sell me a twenty-five million dollar building?'"

Cindy continues, "Sorry, but that's not the way it works. I start in exactly the same position you do. A new contact knows nothing about me and can't distinguish me from anyone else. I start fresh with each new person I meet. It's unrealistic for any of us to think our reputation precedes us. To expect otherwise is to invite disappointment and disillusionment. This will, over time, interfere with your satisfaction and happiness."

What's Cindy's advice? No matter how competent you are, don't count on your good reputation to carry the day. Likewise, approach your new acquaintances with a certain level of skepticism. No individuals, regardless of their accomplishments, are immune from continually having to proving their worth. You cannot trust new people until they earn your trust—and you must earn respect and trust with each new person you meet—no exceptions.

Be Careful What You Wish For

You might dream of untold wealth, but too often when your dream comes true, you have to face more negative consequences than positive ones. For instance, lotteries provide the hope of instant riches—often far beyond the dreams of the ticket purchaser. Yet, rather than experiencing instant happiness, many winners end up broke, depressed, and lonely (Wesley, 2007).

Aristotle says not to expect happiness to be a result of a specific action or change. The stories of lottery winners who suddenly became rich illustrate that money doesn't automatically bring happiness. In fact, some winners have reported feeling *less happy* after winning the money. These winners exemplify the kind of thinking that brought Aristotle to comment that, when a man is poor, he often thinks money will bring happiness (*NE* 1095a20).

Unfortunately, it doesn't necessarily happen that way. And when winning the lottery doesn't evoke the expected happiness, disappointment will likely result.

Eliminating Unrealistic Expectations

How can you eliminate unrealistic expectations? Expect nothing from any particular event, accomplishment, or good deed. Rather, do the right thing for the right person, at the right time, and in the right way. There are no expectations attached because these actions are all about being excellent.

Based on Aristotle's idea, if you act this way, you're leading the kind of life that bears the happiness you desire. That is, a life which avoids most *stoppers*.

Chapter 5: Summary of Concepts

Unrealistic expectations are a common source of disappointment that often occurs when you allow your emotions to determine your actions or you base your actions on faulty assumptions. Beware! Purely emotional responses pose *stoppers* to happiness. It doesn't matter if your expectations relate to business, family, or personal matters. The more rational you are, the more realistic your expectations will be and the greater your chances for happiness.

According to Aristotle, an action is considered virtuous only when it's performed for the right reason. If you do a kind deed for someone solely to get something in return, you aren't performing an action for the right reason.

People often believe that happiness results from a specific action or change for the better. Yet no one change or action can produce deep and continuing satisfaction in your life. For example, simply gaining material goods can bring disappointment if you expected happiness.

Ask, "What kind of activities do I engage in?" If your activities are primarily for relaxation or fun, then you diminish your chances for happiness. According to Aristotle, the kinds of activities that lead to happiness are virtuous and need to include serious actions—not limited to amusement or fun. Relaxation is not the end. Rather, it prepares you for the serious activity you must engage in to attain happiness. Neglecting serious and thoughtful pursuits is another way you create a *stopper* to your happiness.

Points to Think About

1. Unrealistic expectations often lead to disappointment.
2. Disappointment resulting from unrealized expectations is a *stopper.*
3. A good reputation does not precede you. Rather, you start over with each new person you meet.
4. Eliminate the unrealistic expectation that happiness will occur when a particular need is satisfied.
5. If you (or anyone you know) have unrealistic expectations similar to those that Jack and Bob showed, it's wise to identify and avoid them.

Dos and Don'ts

- *Do* the right thing—without any expectation of reciprocation or appreciation.
- *Do* talk to your family and friends about the meaning and value of generosity, including financial charity, acts of forgiveness, and other kinds of generosity.
- *Don't* expect that your competence will be known to anyone.
- *Don't* expect others will respond to your good actions with appreciation.

Take Action

1. Review the reasonableness of your current expectations and think of ways you might adjust them.

2. Describe the experiences you've had when your expectations did not materialize. What lessons did you learn from these experiences?
3. How do your lessons relate to Aristotle's teachings?

"In a complete life, since many changes occur ... the most prosperous may fall into great misfortune."
—Aristotle (*NE* 1100a5)

Chapter 6: Change and Failure

Back in the 1980s, Dan, a professor of business and specialist in strategic planning, foresaw changes taking place in the life insurance industry. Brought about by the newly evolving field of financial planning, these changes would require life insurance agents (and insurance companies) to incorporate securities, real estate, and other unfamiliar elements into their business life. This required new testing, licensing, and training, all of which could be disconcerting to people who had built long-time careers specializing in life insurance.

During this transitional period, Dan accepted a number of speaking engagements at industry gatherings. When asked to comment about his vision of the industry's future, Dan was clear and unambiguous. He believed that the financial future of insurance professionals was endangered by these changes—that is, the industry as it was now organized was heading for extinction. Dan observed that many people in the industry denied the reality of these changes. This denial, he said, made the situation even more dangerous for those who made their living in the industry.

To emphasize his point, Dan compared working in a dying industry to riding on a dying dinosaur. He said, "Those of us who run businesses in this industry are sitting on sick creatures that will soon die. There are dinosaurs dying all around us, and sooner or later, our particular dinosaur will be finished." In response, someone in the audience yelled, "Dinosaurs, as you call them, can't be dying. I can prove this. I'm riding one, and it's fine."

So Dan gave examples of insurance companies that failed and asked, "What about these dead dinosaurs?"

The man simply couldn't accept that things change slowly, nor could he concede that the fact his "dinosaur" hadn't died yet hadn't made his point. The man believed that, because he was fine at the moment, he would be fine forever. Then he pointed his finger at Dan and said, "You, Dan, are spreading negative thoughts that are nothing other than self-fulfilling prophecies."

Change: A Continuing and Inevitable Life Condition

Like the example of the insurance industry, recent events in the automobile industry also show how denial can be destructive.

The auto executives refused to recognize change in their industry. In fact, they were so far removed from rational thinking that they flew to Washington, DC in their private jets to testify before Congress about the financial difficulties their companies were experiencing. These executives took part in wrecking their industry simply by refusing to believe that Japanese-made cars were of higher quality as well as better equipped to meet customer demands. As one commentator put it, "The auto executives didn't know there was a problem until they missed their Christmas bonus." Denying reality is the kind of irrationality that becomes a potential *stopper* to happiness.

Overwhelmed by the fear of negative change, people deny the clues and put their heads in the sand. Lack of acknowledgement coupled with the consequent absence of a reasoned response make it impossible to determine the correct action to take. When you take incorrect action—including no action—a *stopper* is likely to appear.

What happened with the reorganization of both the insurance industry and the automobile industry? People lost their jobs and their personal security. What would have happened if the executives had jumped on the negative clues and responded correctly? It's unknown. But they could have eliminated denial and paid attention to the negative clues, which would have likely led to—

- An accurate examination of the situation.
- A method to discover the mean between excess and deficiency.
- Development of a plan to correctly respond to a developing crisis.

Developing an action plan consistent with the mean (the point between excess and deficiency) would align with the wisest strategy possible. For those who don't respond this way, difficulties only multiply. Ultimately, the absence of rational thought becomes a *stopper* to happiness. When the automobile and insurance executives didn't respond to a worsening business climate, they inadvertently strengthened the continuing downward cycle. As no action or the wrong action continues, time goes by—making the problems more difficult yet to resolve. Inevitably, *stoppers* to happiness show up.

The goal? Recognize negative clues and respond rationally to keep problems from worsening. Those individuals who do are most able to make timely adjustments to their professional and personal lives; they avoid *stoppers.*

Today, along with the automobile industry, the print media industry is undergoing wrenching changes. Because of these changes, people at all levels of the industry are endangered, professionally and personally. In response, some do nothing while others make career changes to electronic formats. Still others change professions entirely. Although change is risky, the early adapters have the best chance for minimum disruption to their careers. That is, they'll have a greater chance to continue and attain the material minimums necessary for happiness.

You know the old proverb "the devil you know is better than the devil you don't know." By the same token, if you don't make changes, the world goes on and you fall behind in your endeavors. Often, doing nothing entails a greater risk than making rational changes using partial or doubtful data—more the rule than the exception. The real world requires you to piece together the clues and decide how to proceed without all the information you'd like to have. Just think about General Eisenhower during World War II. He didn't have a clear weather report, yet he had to decide whether to order the landing of his troops at Normandy Beach to do battle. The general had to *pull the trigger* based on inadequate and undependable information.

The same is true for us. What school should we send our children to? Should we invest in stocks or bonds? These kinds of questions fill our life. They do not, of course, come with an answer sheet. We generally have to *pull the trigger* relying on inadequate and often undependable information.

You might find yourself in a situation like that of the insurance people, the automobile people, or the print media people. Given the circumstances, you can't know how to react to the unpredictable yet vital changes you face. Sometimes you lack necessary information. Sometimes you can't completely understand the changes that swirl around you. You might become paralyzed by an emotional response to the situation.

Regardless of the reasons that inhibit you from dealing with your problems, you have to confront them to make wise decisions.

To be rational, you want to get as much salient information as you can and approach the situation with little emotion.

In many circumstances, such as Darlene's, that's extremely difficult to do.

Darlene knew her marriage was in trouble. Her relationship with her husband, Patrick, was growing increasingly more tense. The silences between them were almost nonstop. At the same time, their business was suffering and bills were piling up. She saw divorce and bankruptcy ahead and had no one to talk to about them. Not only was she afraid to talk to Patrick, she was scared to talk to their creditors. Adding to the unbearable pressure, she questioned if she'd make the problems worse by starting to talk about them. Feeling paralyzed, she knew that by doing nothing, she was making a decision by default.

In Darlene's case—and those like it—a passive response is a decision to do nothing. When you don't confront an issue, you make the most dangerous decision of all. What happens? The issue remains and, over time, the stakes increase. Plus, as the need to decide escalates, so do the chances of acting in a less-than-rational way.

Consider the ability to confront difficult problems and prepare for change as critical skills to learn. This applies to everything in life: relationships, business, family life. Often, tough circumstances present themselves in profound and undesirable ways. Still, you must deal with them in the interest of long-term personal gain.

To best prepare for unwelcome change, stay aware and respond to clues rationally. Then confront whatever challenge appears on the horizon without delay—despite your fears. Most of the time, that problem will catch up to you and hit you on the head.

Effective Optimism

Optimism means seeing the future in favorable terms; pessimism means taking the gloomy view. But note that being aware of negative clues isn't a sign of pessimism. Rather, embracing these negative clues is necessary in carrying out a plan to achieve positive results. Although it might seem counterintuitive, if optimistic people want to avoid *stoppers* resulting from their hopeful outlook, they need to identify and examine negative clues so they can develop effective plans and gain positive results.

These negative clues are often available to us by embracing potentially negative information—that is, being receptive to all the facts whether they represent good news or bad news. That's when we need to be committed to carefully reviewing all the data in the time available. For example, we need to know when profits are down or when the enemy appears strong. Stated simply, we need to stay connected to the reality of the circumstance. This is particularly true when the danger is greatest.

This process requires making an effort to plan responses to problems that may never occur. You can resent this expenditure of energy, but it's necessary to plan for the worst-case scenario. You know the maxim, "Hope for the best and plan for the worst." To have the best chance for a favorable outcome, follow these five steps:

1. Think about the worst thing that could plausibly happen.
2. Develop a plan to attain positive results and avoid negative results.
3. Define the best outcome.
4. Identify the steps to reach the best outcome.
5. Work to overcome the barriers one by one.

Whether human beings are naturally optimistic, pessimistic, or varied has been widely discussed. The core idea is the distinction between feeling optimistic versus doing something that delivers the best chance of achieving the positive result you expect. An effective optimist maximizes the chances for the favorable outcome that's predicted with optimism. Thus, optimistic people are determined to improve their outcomes by preparing for problems before they arrive.

Realize that optimistic thinking differs from "blue sky," careless, naïve, or cavalier thinking. When someone says (for no discernible reason), "Don't worry; everything will be fine," you should worry even more. Why? Because denying the possibility of negative outcomes inevitably invites more negative outcomes—mostly because of lack of preparation. After all, the thinking goes, why be prepared and careful if "everything will be fine" anyway. Yet when bad outcomes occur, they can become *stoppers* to one's happiness.

Failure: A Continuing and Inevitable Life Condition

After failing in his first business attempt, Dale, an entrepreneur in his mid-thirties, is again starting his own company. He describes the new venture to Herb, an older, highly successful executive. Herb reminds Dale of his first venture's failure by saying, "You thought you'd be successful when you tried the first time, but you failed. What makes you think you'll be successful this time?"

Dale then reminds Herb that he, too, has failed a number of times over his career, going on to say, "No one has a life without misfortune or a career with no failures. Our life trajectory is not vertical; it is more like the trajectory of a rocket ship to the moon. Every time it veers off, it needs to be put back on course in order to reach the objective." Dale goes on to say, "We need to learn from our experiences. Generally speaking, I subscribe to the idea that we learn more from our failures than our successes. In my last venture, for instance, I didn't do enough research about the market I wanted to serve. That's a mistake I won't make this time."

Dale, like the rest of us, has had and will continue to have failures in his life. As long as he keeps striving to reach his challenging objectives, he will face possible failures. Aristotle points out that even the best people experience both good and bad fortune. He advises taking life's ups and downs in stride by observing that "a magnanimous person will neither be excessively pleased by good fortune nor excessively distressed by ill fortune" (*NE* 1124a15).

Like most others, you probably enjoy a moderate amount of certainty and predictability—conditions that aren't always available. With or without them, your best defense is embracing change and responding with appropriate action. Dale is one who tries to move ahead every day in the face of possible failure. When you know it's a necessary part of risk-taking, you're better prepared to respond. Part of this involves realizing that, to move into the unknowable future, you have to risk failing. Without taking risks, enjoying rewards based that result from risk-taking are impossible. Indeed, when babies take their first steps, isn't that risk-taking, too?

Embrace the Possibility of Failing

Embracing the possibility of failure better equips you for happiness. Why? Because it makes you less fearful of new and difficult challenges. When you recognize all the possibilities, both positive and negative, you effectively dismantle the *stoppers* to happiness. These *stoppers* should be avoided:

- Inaction because of the fear of failure
- Lack of self-respect because you're afraid to try
- Lack of confidence about a good result

Some believe that *acknowledging* the possibility of failure creates a self-fulfilling prophecy. Are they the same people who think that declaring success is the same as success itself? They say things like "our team will win every game this season" and "every person who reads my book will love it" and "I know it will work this time." These predictions become mindless because they have nothing to do with success or failure. What *is* required to avoid *stoppers* and the best possibility for happiness? Reality-based thinking together with good judgment, proper planning, and execution.

Dale, the entrepreneur who experienced failure, is concerned about failing again as he moves ahead. As time passes, however, he will either need to lead his business to success or take a job working for someone else. Consider this: if Dale's new business fails and he has to move on, this failure isn't evidence of an unsuccessful or unhappy life. Dale would persist in learning from it and moving ahead to something new.

In any case, just about any failure is a failed *endeavor* that doesn't preclude moving on to other endeavors. Indeed, failed endeavors result from an active life—the kind of life Aristotle recommends for happiness (*NE* 1098b30). The best attitude is focusing on preparing for the next battle. Thomas Edison, renowned for trying different materials in his inventions, searched persistently for the right filament to create the light bulb. He's famous for saying, "I never failed. I just found ten thousand ways that it won't work."

An important benefit results from embracing the possibility of failure—that is, being prepared to rebound when, for example, you don't get the promotion you expect, or you lose the championship game, or you fail a licensing exam. Remember, these failures have nothing to do with your character or general competence. Having clarity about this allows you to move on to face your next challenge. You know other promotions, games, and exams will come your way.

Dale can take comfort knowing he's following advice provided by a great philosopher. As prescribed by Aristotle, he is—

- In a state of pursuit and investigation.
- Thinking about the right thing to do and the right time to do it.
- Knowing there is a risk of failure

To be happy, reality-based, thoughtful activity is required. So are the inevitable failures along the way. As Aristotle says, the function of a man is "an activity of the soul in conformity with a rational principle" (NE 1098a9).

Look for the Negative Clues

Stanton, a business professor and specialist in strategic planning, serves on the board of Charlie's company. Charlie confesses to Stanton that he often feels uncertain about his business decisions. Charlie has serious concerns about what strategy to follow, what changes to make, how to invest, whom to hire and fire, and so on. Charlie shares that he often feels the need to take action but can't get an accurate read on what is going on. Stanton advises, "Look at the clues that are all around you. They'll give you hints about what's likely to occur."

Searching for negative clues is critical for taking action preemptively. They're the kinds of clues the automobile executives appear to have ignored.

Negative clues serve as warning signs about potential changes in our environment. As Stanton said, they're all around us. For example, Al Gore presents scientific data about global warming as clues to the future, assuring his listeners that there are enough clues to move them to action. Often, when a large, uncertain threat looms, the natural response is to deny its existence. Yet, even with uncertainty, the bigger the threat, the more attention should be paid to it.

If you do a good job of watching out for negatives, you can be more optimistic about avoiding *stoppers*. Remember, when you're faced with important decisions, the less emotion the better. Emotions and beliefs, though important, should be independent of good decision-making. Can you think of a group of individuals who have opposing beliefs and emotions about an issue but must make a decision about it? Any decision made will be against the beliefs or emotions of some individuals within the group. Yet, when people get emotional, their perceptions can be distorted. It's wise for intelligent people to demand that their reason control their emotions. As Aristotle says, "emotions are not under the control of reason unless we insist upon it being so" (*NE* 1102b15).

Limits on Predictability

You can evaluate a spreadsheet or measure a table with precision. But, as noted in Chapter 1, it's difficult to be precise with topics like happiness and other critical aspects of living. For example, you can't predict with certainty whether a business or career will succeed, when you will die, if your children will do well, or whether your marriage will last a long time. Not being able to predict things in life can be quite upsetting.

Usually, you can protect yourself against *stoppers* resulting from negative change by evaluating the clues—both negative and positive. These clues help you predict outcomes and prepare for the future. As noted earlier in this chapter, the negative clues are the more important ones to address because doing so might protect you from threat or danger. And using the positive clues around you can give you reason for optimism.

Sledgehammer Words: *Stoppers* to Optimism and Rationality

Ever heard or said the following statements?

- "I can't do this."
- "I have to do that."
- "We must have this."
- "You shouldn't have done that!"

Uttered either internally or externally, these statements are certain to be a source of resentment and unhappiness. They come crashing down with all the subtlety of a sledgehammer, leaving fear and inertia in their wake.

Sledgehammer words and thoughts inflict damage in matters big and small. Here are a few more examples:

- "I'll never get another job with the market as it is."
- "I mustn't even think about the negative possibilities."

When the stakes get higher, you might hear:

- "I need to stay with my husband, even though he abuses me."
- "I must remain in this business relationship, even though it wears me down."

Individuals with a "can't do" or "must do" habit think they have no options for changing what they want to change. The truth is, there's almost always an option, even if it requires choosing from a series of unpleasant choices. You could, for example, leave your spouse or business partner and accept the negative emotional and financial consequences. You'd still be exercising your power to choose. Don't think like a slave; know that you have more options than you think. And you have the power to choose.

When you conclude that you're trapped by what you believe you "can't do" or "must do," you've established a *stopper* to your happiness. You see, an unhappy individual perceives that life happens *to* him or her, no choices available. However, if feelings of entrapment are removed and options recognized, *this one step* significantly increases one's chances for happiness.

Deciding which action to take requires rational evaluation. If you have already concluded that you have no options, there is no action decision needed. Therefore, evaluation is no longer useful. When you find yourself in that emotional state, it's important to remember that you have decided the right action to take is no longer yours to choose. However, if it's important to you to remain in control of your action decisions, avoid self-destructive thoughts such as "*I can't*" or "*I must.*" If you're unable to control your emotions, it might be helpful to speak with friends or even a professional to get back on track.

Chapter 6: Summary of Concepts

Negative news and change are a part of life. You have these choices: to accept or deny, to adjust, or to remain the same.

Coming up with a good response to events requires responding *rationally.* That requires taking thoughtful action when facing uncertainty, even if your research is incomplete. When you respond emotionally to unwelcome news, you can feel overwhelmed or anxious. In that event, search for all clues and signals that exist. Sure, you might feel more comfortable if you have certainty and precision in your life. But this isn't reality. With the world around you constantly changing, don't expect certainty or precision. Just know that you enhance your chances for happiness when you're optimistic. You "hope for the best" while rationally "planning for the worst."

Any pursuit contains the possibility of failure. If you can accept this fact, you can take on challenges that are increasingly more difficult. However, this isn't a prediction of failure. Look for the emotional freedom to pursue projects that might fail. Remember, you can continue to pursue success without feeling bad or inadequate even if you don't get a good result. Imagine scientists unwilling to accept the risk that their experiments might fail. Avoiding the possibility of failure requires giving up the possibility of success. Eliminating all risk of failure can give birth to a *stopper* to happiness.

To avoid *stoppers* to your happiness, embrace rather than resist the negative clues in your environment. These negative clues are often early warning signs of change. As you look for what action to take, schedule time to distinguish reality from emotion so you make wise decisions. Use words that describe a situation accurately and rationally rather than emotionally. Many people tend to freeze when changes are serious and unexpected. It's best to decide on an action to take—and take it! Deciding not to act is still a form of action, after all.

Points to Think About

1. A person who plans for negative possibilities is not being a pessimist.
2. Failed endeavors help ground you in reality, which in turn improves subsequent decision-making.
3. Failed endeavors are a critical part of life experience.
4. Sledgehammer words trigger emotions; their use is a *stopper.*
5. An effective optimist does not typically say, "Everything will be fine."
6. Refusal to accept life's inevitable changes is a *stopper.*
7. Refusal to face new challenges is a *stopper.*

Dos and Don'ts

- *Do* view change as an inevitable part of life.
- *Do* view failure as a necessary part of risk-taking, allowing you to stretch.
- *Do* look for and take action to deal with the negative clues that emerge.
- *Don't* avoid looking for negative clues.
- *Don't* view optimism as only looking for the positives.
- *Don't* allow lack of precision to dissuade you from doing the right thing at the right time.

Take Action

1. What are your natural reactions to unwelcome change? Are your responses typically different at work than they are at home? Describe your reaction to the following:
    - Unwelcome change at work.
    - Unwelcome change at home.
    - Unexpected change in your community or the world at large.
2. Can you identify an incident when you hoped for the best and planned for the worst and the worst happened?
    - Name the event or situation.
    - What were the results and consequences?
3. Can you identify an incident in which you *neglected* to plan for the worst and the worst happened?
    - Name the event or situation.
    - Were the results and consequences worse than they would have been if you had made a plan? How?

"There are some things, the lack of which takes away the luster from happiness."
—Aristotle (*NE* 1099b4)

Chapter 7: Irresolvable Problems

Carl, a successful and ethical professional, had been married to Sharon for twenty-two years before they divorced. Their twenty-year-old daughter, Dana, is working and financially independent. Dana describes Carl and Sharon as "good parents." She adds, however, that since the divorce, her mother could be depressed. She lies around most of the day and seems incapable of getting her life together. Dana constantly worries about Sharon and the fact that she doesn't have the financial or emotional resources to help her mother.

In speaking to her father about her concerns, Dana finds that Carl has no feeling of responsibility toward Sharon. His ex-wife's difficulties have nothing to do with him. As far as he's concerned, while he wants to do the right thing for all concerned, the divorce and corresponding financial settlement ended his responsibilities to Sharon. He has put his relationship with Sharon behind him forever.

Difficult Permanent Relationships

It seems reasonable to think that ending a relationship ends the problems within the relationship. In the case of divorce, presumably once all the children of the marriage are grown, there is no need for any continuing relationship or communication. The divorced couple settles whatever needs settling, explains the situation to the rest of the family, and moves on. This seems clear, but still, a surprising number of situations require continuing communication.

Carl errs by concluding that, when the divorce is final, his responsibility to Sharon ends. This results from Carl wanting Dana to do the right thing—to help her mother as best she can. And to be a "good" father, Carl needs to help Dana. The result? Carl has an unexpected, unwelcome, and continuing—possibly permanent—obligation to assist his daughter in helping his ex-wife.

For Carl, discovering that he could never be completely free of his ex-wife's problems had the potential to be a *stopper* to his happiness. The problem he thought of as *irresolvable* can be solved by recognizing that his responsibility to his daughter includes whatever problems come her way—Sharon included, just like any other problem.

This kind of unwanted, unchangeable relationship is common. Take the example of siblings who don't get along. Often within the family dynamic, siblings are compelled to be together, notwithstanding any personal difficulties. Common familial relationships including parents and other family members make it hard to end the sibling relationship. The family congregates for one thing or another, with no one willing to give up territory. When brothers and sisters refuse to speak to each other or even be in the same room, it presents a much more complex situation than if two unrelated people had the same problem with each other.

Business partners can present another type of potentially difficult relationship. People start a company and become financially entwined in such a way they can't extricate themselves. When the personal relationship becomes intolerable and the partners want to terminate their relationship, it's easier said than done. Ending the relationship could mean destroying their business and the way they earn their living.

What's the common denominator in these examples? It is the inability to change or end relationships when they're no longer desired. Most likely, you're in a permanent relationship of one kind or another such as a parent, child, sibling, business partner, or life partner. When permanent relationships like these aren't welcome, they feel like irresolvable problems that won't go away. When siblings have relationship problems, they often avoid dealing with the fact that they're attached for life on some level. Siblings can't easily avoid their common problems (e.g., dealing with aging parents) or family occasions. They need to get along (or have an agreed understanding) to avoid the anxiety that comes from having an unwelcome common purpose.

In the case of business, when a partnership begins, the partners envision a permanent relationship over a long time. Like a marriage, they intend to go through thick and thin together. This kind of relationship can sometimes be harder to terminate than a marriage.

How can Carl, the siblings, and the business partners solve their so-called "irresolvable problem" and rid themselves of a potential *stopper* to their happiness? The solution is for each of them to focus on the wisest action to take.

It's natural to sometimes feel anger or disappointment toward others. These emotions, however, shouldn't be allowed to direct any actions. Carl needs to recognize that his responsibility to Dana necessarily includes her responsibility to her mother. In the same way, brothers and sisters have to deal with the problems that accompany unchangeable family connections and commitments. In both cases, a rational approach lessens the possibility of problems becoming *stoppers* to happiness.

Emotional Responses to Potential *Stoppers*

Innumerable situations can cause an emotional reaction that acts as a *stopper* as well, including:

- Divorce
- Loss of a job
- Loss of a home
- Financial crisis
- Onset of a serious illness
- Conflicts or difficulties with others

All these experiences are potential *stoppers* to happiness based on emotional responses. It's critical, therefore, to refuse to allow these emotions to overwhelm you and take control of your rational thought. What's your best chance of overcoming adversity and avoiding a *stopper?* Using reason to control or manage your emotions—no matter what the crisis might be.

Remaining rational in the face of strong emotion can be accomplished. Soldiers in battle provide an example for us. If soldiers in the line of action want to stay alive, they need to make rational decisions while experiencing extreme emotions. They're often forced to make these rational decisions in times of great emotional stress.

In the military arena, in the short term, soldiers have learned to control their emotions through their training. But in the long term, after they survive the do-or-die situations, a soldier's emotions must be addressed, often with the assistance of experts. Inadequately facing many kinds of trauma can result in post-traumatic stress disorder (PTSD).

Financial Crisis

In recent years, the United States and much of the world experienced a devastating economic crash. Millions of people who had nothing to do with causing the crisis suffered terrible financial hardships. Getting caught up in unfixable financial circumstances presented them with unavoidable potential *stoppers* to their happiness—predicaments that could last a lifetime.

Many people, though, will experience a full or partial recovery as they find a new way to make a living (even if it's for less money than they previously made). Before the crash, people were buying big cars and fancy new kitchens. After the crash, they adjusted their thinking and now buy a used car and a house that meets their family's minimum financial requirements. Although many have less wealth than before the crisis, they still have the minimums necessary for happiness.

Consider a situation in which you no longer can afford the cost of living in a large home. If your job provides enough income to support your family in a small apartment, there's no reason to think happiness can't be yours. Living in an apartment (as opposed to a house) is not the kind of loss that has to be a *stopper*. After all, life brings changes—good, bad, and worse.

According to the *New York Times*, "During this period of deep recession, people quietly but noticeably have refigured their lives to elevate experiences over things" (Cave, 2010). The same article reported that a recent *New York Times*/CBS poll found that nearly half of Americans said they were spending less time buying nonessentials and more than half were spending less money in stores and online. Although some worked longer hours, a larger portion of the population was spending additional time with their family and friends. Again, these people can retain their happy lives, having less in the way of material goods.

A *stopper* can occur when you lose sight of the fact that happiness is attainable. Don't believe for a second that what you possess now is required for happiness. In most cases, even in the midst of difficulty, you still retain the minimum needed. Certainly economic reversals (as opposed to catastrophes) don't have to be *stoppers* to happiness.

Mortality

Professor Thomas tells about a journalist, Cheryl, who had a near-death experience. After Cheryl recovered, she wrote about her experience. Upon waking, she found herself lying in a comfortable bed in a very nice room. Several people there were attending to her every need. Some wore medical clothing and others, including family members, wore street clothes. In addition to treating her medically, they fed and bathed her and took her to the bathroom as if she were a baby. Cheryl needed and appreciated the help.

Cheryl explained her perception of what she experienced in that hospital room. The people helping her appeared confident in their strength as if they were permanently strong and she was permanently weak. In a vague kind of way, they seemed unaware of their own future weakness and ultimate mortality. They didn't understand that it was her turn in the bed this time; next time it would be theirs.

How could the people caring for Cheryl not know (or want to know) that, in time, they'd also get their turn to be in "the bed"? Perhaps these caregivers didn't see any benefit from being reminded of their inability to stop their own movements toward "the bed." However, if these people think denying reality helps them, they are mistaken—especially when the unexpected happens, such as the death of a child.

Unexpected Tragedy

Is there any way to intellectually or emotionally prepare for the sudden, unexpected, and unpredictable death of a loved one?

Janet's son, Phillip, a thirty-eight-year-old husband and father, died after having a ski accident—a result of random bad luck. No one, including Phillip, was held responsible for his death. Janet, ordinarily a resilient, competent, and happy person, said Phillip's death brought her to her "emotional knees." She allowed herself to experience the pain of the "worst loss imaginable," while slowly but actively working on her ability to deal with the loss. She reached out for grief counseling, support groups, and the loving kindness of family and friends, and accessed her natural resilience.

Notwithstanding her efforts, Janet thought her grief would never diminish enough for happiness to be possible again. However, some years later, Janet has recovered enough to enjoy her time with her wonderful family members. Her life is again full of worthwhile activities. She views herself as forever changed; a still pained but happy person.

Aristotle says we are less likely to be happy without good family and friends. We are even less likely to be happy if we lose children, family, or friends by death (*NE* 1099b1). These losses may be so devastating that they diminish or eliminate the possibility of happiness (*NE* 1099b4).

This is what happened to Janet and her family when Phillip was killed. As discussed in Chapter 2, bad luck plays a part in our chances for happiness. Fortunately, Janet's been able to recover from this devastating loss. While she admits there's a permanent "empty seat at the table" feeling, she says she has diminished what for many would be a permanent *stopper*.

Martin Heidegger, a German philosopher, argues that death is a constant presence in life. He renames human existence as "being toward death" and asks, "What is human existence, if not a limited stretch from birth to death? Human existence is marked by finitude and limitation, and those of us who ignore this fact are engaged in a futile pursuit, trying to escape the inescapable." To understand fully, Heidegger argues, one must understand oneself as finite (Being and Time, 1962). Some people try (hopelessly) to take comfort by denying their mortality. Others are continually aware of their mortality and use this awareness to gain a greater insight into the human condition.

Once you are aware of your finite existence, you can avoid certain *stoppers* to happiness. Chapter 1 explained the relationship between reasoned thinking, intelligence, and excellence. Understanding your own and others' mortality is a critical part of reasoned thinking. Inevitably, this understanding plays a part in calculating the decisions you make—the decisions about the right thing to do, the person to do it for, the right time to do it, and the right reason for doing it.

A Beautiful Plan

Warren, a middle-aged businessman, had Lou Gehrig's disease. Although once physically strong, fit, healthy, and enthusiastic, he was slowly losing his ability to move and becoming increasingly more disabled. Soon he'd be confined to a wheelchair and, as the disease progressed, would further suffer its debilitating symptoms.

Warren stated two things he wanted to do before he couldn't move around on his own. The first—to finish constructing the home he and his wife had been building for years. The second—to determine the time and means of his death. He didn't want to go through the tragic process in store for him, nor did he want his family to be subjected to it.

Warren decided the best plan was to commit suicide. He knew that to be successful in controlling when to end his life, he had to take action before he was completely disabled. He succeeded as planned, completing his house and ending his life on his own timeline.

Warren's death was certainly a tragedy for those he left behind. Undoubtedly, the death of a loved one could be the worst kind of a *stopper* to happiness. Whether you ethically agree with suicide or not,

Warren's act of committing suicide was his attempt at being thoughtful to the end of his life—his idea of the right thing to do, both in his own best interests and the best interests of those he loved. Warren concluded that, because he had an irresolvable problem (his disease), he could spend the last part of his life doing what he could about what mattered to him. He was concerned about his family, his home, and—most important—being excellent until the end. Once his diagnosis and prognosis were certain, Warren didn't spend much time thinking about the illness itself. As Aristotle has said, "There's no point in thinking too much about what cannot be changed. A wise man thinks about what he can do something about" (NE 1141b9). Even at his impending death, Warren allowed no one thing to dominate all others in his concern.

Turning to Philosophy in Turbulent Times

Philosophical thinking isn't a "magic bullet." However, philosophy can provide a strong way of thinking about the management of expectations and the minimum requirements for happiness. For these reasons, Aristotle's philosophy is particularly valuable especially during turbulent times. The recent economic downturn has compelled many people to review their thoughts about the relationship of material goods to happiness. Rational thinking greatly helps because it's important to be able to differentiate the real from the imagined *stoppers.* That is, it's important to distinguish between the kind of severe negative economic changes that are a danger to happiness and those changes that leave us "lesser" than before.

There is, for example, a big difference between (a) being in the middle of the desert with no water and no hope and (b) *thinking or fearing* you're in the middle of the desert when you're actually near an (unseen) road and two miles from a gas station. At first glance, the two look and feel the same. There is, however, a world of difference. In circumstance (a), you have an irresolvable problem that you must reconcile. In circumstance (b), you have a problem that *appears* to be irresolvable. The critical ability is being able to rationally determine which is real, (a) or (b).

Chapter 1 noted Aristotle's view that part of the human mind operates from emotion independently from reason. Emotions can be positive or negative. In any case, you need to put them aside (even for a moment) to think through problems rationally. When a problem presents itself, using your reasoning skills will give you the best chances for a positive outcome. Indeed, Aristotle thinks reason is necessary for excellence and happiness. By thinking through and implementing a good plan, you (1) manage your emotions so you're more able to reason well and (2) watch for problems you *mistakenly* think of as irresolvable. Indeed, *not* managing your emotions can become a self-fulfilling *stopper* to happiness.

Chapter 7: Summary of Concepts

Many people have difficulties accepting events or conditions they can't control. The reality of life is that, regardless of how competently you manage your life, you run into problems that neither you nor anyone else can solve. Irresolvable problems can include a devastating loss of a job, an illness, or a death of a loved one.

Clearly, you can't control the outcome of many important things that happen, nor can you control the behavior of others toward you or any bad luck that might come your way. No one avoids life's irresolvable problems. With no philosophic framework to guide you, your emotions will rule in the face of difficulty. When that happens, happiness can easily elude you. On the other hand, using philosophical tools can help you make rational decisions that assist in avoiding unhappiness.

Acknowledging and embracing your mortality can assist in pursuing happiness. Being aware of your mortality lets you think rationally and maintain focus on your values and goals. Mortality also keeps you connected with reality and helps avoid *stoppers*—thus enhancing your chance to enjoy sustained satisfaction, contentment, and happiness.

Points to Think About

1. If your problems are severe and permanent, happiness may be unattainable.
2. Be careful when you conclude a problem is irresolvable. Many solutions appear to be beyond reach but can be found using careful reasoning.
3. Being conscious of your mortality can contribute to achieving happiness.
4. Many terminated relationships involve permanent, residual responsibilities.
5. When you feel overwhelmed by "irresolvable problems," consider whether a different perspective or philosophic assumption would help make the problem more acceptable or manageable.

Dos and Don'ts

- *Do* use Aristotle's philosophy to help accept and deal with irresolvable problems.
- *Do* give thought to the issues and your feelings about perceived irresolvable problems you confront.
- *Do* consider the "right thing to do" at all times.
- *Don't allow* your emotions to direct your responses to problems you face.
- *Don't* ignore the way your actions might create irresolvable problems for others.

Take Action

1. Recall and reflect on people you knew who dealt with a terminal illness or other grave situation. Did they deal with their mortality in an intelligent way, as described in this chapter?
2. Reflect upon your experiences with seemingly "irresolvable problems." In what ways did you successfully deal with them? In what ways did your actions reflect rational thinking and controlled emotions?

"Virtue makes us aim at the right target, and practical wisdom makes us take the right means."
—Aristotle (*NE* 1144a7)

Chapter 8: Steps toward Happiness

An up-and-coming professional, Gary was the assistant manager of an insurance agency in Detroit. Tony, the manager to whom he reported, was his mentor. In the course of his management duties, Tony often chatted with the insurance agents and offered them advice on issues that might be bothering them. They enjoyed coming into Tony's office to talk about the big sale they just booked, the big sale they lost, or the troubles they experienced in their personal lives.

One day, a sales representative walked into the office and told both Gary and Tony about his son being diagnosed with a form of cancer, saying he very possibly could die soon. Although Tony did a good job of comforting the father, by the time he'd left, both Gary and Tony were quite upset about the boy's illness.

Shortly after that, another sales representative came in excited about a big sale she wanted to close. Without missing a beat, Tony began discussing effective sales strategies to help her close the sale.

In due course, other reps came into Tony's office to ask about one thing or another. In spite of the lively conversation, Gary could not stop thinking and worrying about the kid who had cancer. It's worth noting that Tony's a straight talker and an acutely smart individual.

Gary wondered about his boss with thoughts like, "If he cared about those people, he couldn't possibly talk about one agent's big sale just after he heard the other guy talking about a dying son. Perhaps all he really cares about is keeping people in place so they continue making sales."

But Gary didn't blurt out his pessimistic thoughts. Instead, he asked Tony, "How can you talk about an agent's big sale after hearing about another's dying son?"

A moment went by, and then Tony asked, "Do you have a television at home?"

Gary said, "Yes."

He said, "Do you have Channel 2?"

"Yes," Gary replied.

"Do you have Channel 4?"

"Yes," Gary replied again.

His next words changed Gary's outlook forever: "Do you ever wonder what happens to Channel 2 when you put on Channel 4?"

At this point, Tony had Gary's full attention. Tony went on, "Imagine being the president of the United States. Just visualize it. You get up in the morning at the White House, you drink your coffee, and then you walk downstairs to the Oval Office. Immediately, your national security advisor comes in and gives you the daily security report. She starts with an update about US citizens who are endangered by rioting in Africa. Next, you hear about an economic meltdown in Spain and a conflict in India. As she comes to the end of her briefing, she tells you all hell is breaking loose at the United Nations. As the national security adviser leaves, your domestic adviser arrives to make his morning report. He says, 'Well, our signature bill is being reviewed by the Supreme Court. I think we're in trouble.' He

> *leaves and the next staffer comes in followed by six or seven others. Each of them has a litany of problems that need to be dealt with by you here and now. From morning until night, you're confronted by people presenting one layer of difficulty after another, piled up to the sky. Any normal human being would collapse under all this pressure. No one can carry that kind of weight.*
>
> *"The good news is you don't* have *to carry it. Like television channels, you have an infinite number you can listen to—one channel for each subject."*

Tony's action allowed him to successfully deal with a multiplicity of ends. He separated issues into different channels or compartments in his mind. This ability to separate allowed him to keep his focus on problems that came at him—one at a time.

Action Step 1: Construct Channels

This story about how Tony constructed channels can help you understand the need for intensity of focus, plus help you optimize your chances for happiness.

When Aristotle says you need to have multiple objectives (ends) for happiness, he implies a need to manage those multiple ends—in modern-day terms, to change channels. Otherwise, you may have a *stopper* to your happiness. Without having a disciplined system, focusing on even one thing for any period is difficult and focusing on *more than* one complex thing at a time is impossible. This is true even for those who pride themselves in being multitaskers.

Research continues to support the idea that doing (or thinking about) more than one thing at a time is unworkable. For example, almost a decade ago, Sandra Blakeslee confirmed what many know intuitively. She said, "You can't do two complex tasks simultaneously as well as you could do either one alone. Previous research has shown that when an area of the brain, like the visual cortex, has to do two things at once, like tracking two objects, there is less brain activation that occurs when it watches one thing at a time" (Blakeslee 2001). You need all of your brainpower when analyzing and solving problems. Therefore, when you're engaged in complex thinking, focus on one thing at a time.

Focus and Rational Thought: Critical Factors

Of course, in some circumstances, pinpointed focus isn't necessary while in other circumstances, total focus is critical to being effective.

> *Imagine you're in the kitchen making soup and at the same time talking to a friend. Perhaps, if you're simply stirring the soup, you can pay full attention to your friend. However, if it boils over, everything changes and you need to turn your full attention to the soup—neglecting your friend.*

When an activity is automatic and mechanical, you can quickly alter your focus and complete tasks relatively well. However, when any kind of complexity or relationship is involved, you need to focus on one thing at a time.

If you insist on taking all of your problems and setting them on top of one another, eventually they'll become *stoppers* and crush you with their weight. On the other hand, if you choose, you can compartmentalize. Like television channels, each one has a huge capacity for receiving and storing information.

In your life, you can build multiple channels—for example, you can build a channel for each of your children, your spouse, each sibling, your business partner, and anyone else. Changing channels lets you redirect your focus completely on a new subject—that is, upon the command of your reasoned thought to your emotions you redirect your focus.

Having a strong ability to "channel change" will enhance your effectiveness so you can:

- Ask necessary and relevant questions.
- Listen more intently.
- Retain more information.
- Retrieve information more easily.

All of your relationships and life events are subject to your internal system of prioritization. For example, you could agree that the typical relationship between a man and his wife is more important than the relationship between a man and a good friend. However, when the friend has a problem, at that moment, you can choose to give the same amount of attention to your friend as you would to your spouse. At a particular moment, your intensity of focus doesn't depend on its ranking on your priority list. At *that* moment of focus, your friend's problem is the only subject of priority interest.

The importance of a particular personal relationship or subject might not be relevant at the time of focus. However, considering you have physical time limits, you must choose which people and issues should receive any channel of your time at all.

Inevitably, you'll replace channels on which you place a low priority. Learning to use channels and avoid "layering up" of problems enhances your ability to manage a multiplicity of ends. After all, happiness depends on multiple ends and doing the right thing for the right person.

Without clarity of thought for "channel changing" from one issue to another, you'll find that happiness is difficult to attain. Even though simple circumstances don't require total focus, remember that when "the soup boils over," everything changes. You need to tell yourself and your friend you have a greater need to focus on "the soup." What do you do?

- Tell your friend you suddenly can't focus on what's being said.
- Change channels to focus on the "boiling over soup."
- Return to your friend as soon as possible.

It's necessary to discipline yourself to (1) channel your issues to avoid feeling overwhelmed and (2) maintain an intensity of focus on the issue of the moment. If you insist on allowing your life's problems to pile up, one atop the other, then you'll be less clear-headed and, consequently, less able to correctly choose the right thing to do.

In today's frenetic, pressured world, it's common to experience "troubles." Tapping into the support of trusted friends and family—or perhaps seeking the counsel of experts—might be useful. For many people, brief, results-oriented counseling helps them unravel a complicated and confusing situation, especially when it involves a loss, a tragedy, or serious financial reversal. Sometimes, the right thing to do is this: Consider what to do for yourself first to aid in dealing with special circumstances. Do you see how using intelligence to consider the right thing for you to do is a precursor for excellence and happiness?

Fuzziness

Certainly on a day-to-day basis, most people know the feeling of mental "fuzziness" when they're engaged in a conversation while thinking about an unrelated problem. Would you be thrilled to be able to forget the last issue and be more focused on the next? Yes! Choosing and acting on the right thing to do is at risk when you feel "fuzzy."

No matter what the subject, learn to change channels completely (letting the second person know you can't focus on right now). This permits you to participate more effectively in whatever is happening *at that moment.* By successfully changing channels, you'll hear the issue more clearly. Then you can ask the necessary questions and retain information for later. Know that, if you put the second person "on hold" until you can fully focus, your conversation will be more successful.

Naturally, when you feel worried about your partner or spouse, it takes discipline to switch channels to your child or other family issues. When you're having personal problems, it takes even more discipline to switch channels to your work. The moment you *decide* to change channels, however, the new subject becomes the only subject in your life. When you learn to change channels quickly, you'll better manage an unlimited number of complex issues.

Because people can feel overwhelmed much or all of the time, Tony models a successful "mind system" to control the "fuzziness" that results from problems piling up. You help yourself by changing channels so you can easily move from emotional to rational thinking.

Building a Wall of Happiness

Joan describes a conversation she has with Marilyn, her thirty-eight-year-old daughter. Challenged in her career, Marilyn wants a change. Joan tries to convince her to return to college and complete her degree program. Marilyn resists, telling Joan she doesn't know if she can successfully do the work and fears the other students are younger and more capable than she is. Her confidence down, she's honestly afraid school will result in another life failure, that it could easily be a waste of time and money. It would be long and difficult and the result, after all that effort, could be that there were no better jobs available to her when she was through. She views it as too much risk.

Joan responds to her daughter by saying, "First, it's true you might not be able to compete with the younger students. Second, it's true you might not have the confidence necessary to be successful. Third, it's true you might wind up with another failure; and fourth, it's true that, when you successfully complete your degree, there might not be any better jobs available to you. All true. On the other hand, if you don't go to school because you think you will fail, you're certain to fail because you didn't try."

Joan goes on to say, "Marilyn, your fears are understandable. Yet you can take action that will give you a chance to reach your objective. Don't dwell on your fears. Concentrate on your rational thought and the possible positive results. For starters, enroll in only one class, any class you'd like. Don't worry about graduating down the road. Just limit your concern to completing this one class. When you do, then you can decide if you want to take another class. After completing the second class, you can decide if you want to take still another. Just keep going as far as you can—at a pace that feels comfortable for you.

"Think of each class you take as one brick in a brick wall you want to build—a wall so ambitious, you realize you may not succeed completing it. That's right. Don't worry about completion. Set each completed brick down, one on top of the other. Take pleasure from doing your best with each brick and remember, don't look back. And never compare your work with anyone else's.

"Chances are, one day you'll turn around and see you've built a wall. Not only will you accomplish a goal, but you will enjoy satisfaction."

The message that Joan gives her daughter offers the greatest chance for Marilyn's ultimate happiness. By advising her daughter to find the right thing to do and then do it, she's consistent with Aristotle's comment "happiness is to be a virtuous activity of the soul, of a certain kind" (*NE* 1099b26). When people are morally virtuous, they try to do the right thing, for the right person, for the right reason, and at the right time. In this case, Joan believes Marilyn is the right person, going back to school is the right thing, and now is the right time.

The mother also advises her daughter to build a wall brick by brick by taking one class at a time. This allows Marilyn to work on her goals in a balanced way without overloading herself with a full-time job during the day and a full-time load of classes at night. That would likely become a *stopper*.

Consider each activity in your life a brick in a wall. Laying down each brick successfully is a valuable path to pursue in and of itself. In combination with all other bricks—multiple, lesser, self-sufficient ends—each brick helps form a wall. Your wall of happiness represents the highest goal and the final self-sufficient end.

Naturally, you value a number of things in your life, including you're your family, profession, friends, health, and so on. Think of each of these as an important brick in your wall. None of these bricks, no matter how important they are, can individually constitute a wall. Rather, each is subordinate to your wall and part of the totality of the bricks.

If you want to build a wall of happiness, you will need to—

- Know how to make or acquire bricks.
- Collect all the bricks and organize them in manner consistent with a plan.
- Lay each brick in an excellent (virtuous) way as Aristotle defines excellence. It needs to be done on a mean between extremes.

If you limit yourself to one aspect of wall building by becoming an expert on the "chemistry of bricks" or "the esthetics of walls" or even "the construction of walls," you'll never complete the wall. Meshing all your activities constitutes your effort to build an excellent wall. Happy people tend to put all the important components of their life together and find the balance they need to make an excellent wall.

Remember, the best walls are built when focusing on one brick at a time.

Understandably, it's not easy to give one brick all your attention when many others command it, too. The solution? Construct different channels in your mind, just as Tony did. This stops you from feeling overwhelmed and collapsing under layers of problems. Act with excellence as you engage in each activity independent of the others. The intent is, without overwhelming yourself, to establish each of your ends as an independent and unique entity (a brick) that becomes part of your wall of happiness. The sum of all your work allows you to manage a multiplicity of ends with excellence of each. To achieve this, a tremendous amount of discipline is necessary.

You use discipline to (1) avoid feeling overwhelmed by channeling your issues and (2) be excellent in your performance. Forget about multitasking. Focus on concepts like seeking the mean between excess and deficiency, pursuing a multiplicity of ends, and considering the degree to which your expectations are realistic.

All this requires you to set aside time frequently to focus on how you will pursue happiness in your life.

Chapter 8: Summary of Concepts

Three tools help you apply some of Aristotle's teaching to your daily life. The first involves the concept of layers and channels to assist in managing a multiplicity of ends. As you consider this concept, use your rational abilities to avoid "layering up" issues in your life.

You can move from channel to channel focusing on the one issue that needs your immediate attention at one time. Having the ability to change channels gives you a sense of being able to control the challenges that confront you without feeling overwhelmed.

The second tool, the concept of your "wall of happiness," allows you to envision each aspect of your life separately and to work toward excellence in each. Combining excellent bricks contributes to building an excellent wall. Although you have a multiplicity of ends, you will succeed by dealing with one issue or challenge at a time.

The third tool is your conscious effort to focus on doing the types of activities viewed as virtuous and doing these in a balanced manner. This involves consciously focusing on the tasks required to attain happiness. Concentrate on what you do and commit to doing one thing at a time. In this manner, you'll keep the *stoppers* from thwarting your attempts to attain happiness.

When you remain focused, you'll have a better chance of identifying the right thing to do and acting on that knowledge. Only with focus can you move from Aristotle's definition of *true intelligence* to his definition of *excellence.*

Use the concept of layers and channels as a street-smart method of organizing a multiplicity of ends and avoiding overwhelm. Why is that important? When you become overwhelmed, your emotion stops you from achieving happiness. The better you can construct channels (rather than layer concerns), the better your chances of managing a large number of activities.

Each channel represents a part of the kind of person you want to be, pursuing each end with intelligence and excellence while building a solid wall of happiness brick by brick. This concept ties in with developing the discipline to use your ability to focus on diverse, important issues—a tool that's critical for good decision-making and for applying Aristotle's philosophy to attain happiness.

Points to Think About

1. Most people have more issues in their lives than they can handle unless they acquire the ability to deal with them one at a time.
2. If you refuse to allow issues to "layer up," you become more effective at everything you do.
3. If you do every particular thing with excellence, you remove *stoppers* and increase your chances for happiness. Attempt to do every activity with care and forethought.

Dos and Don'ts

- *Do* use the concept of layers and channels to focus on a particular issue at a particular moment in time. This will help as you pursue a multiplicity of ends.
- *Do* use the concept of a "wall of happiness" to work on one issue at a time.
- *Don't* think about one thing while you are engaged in another; focus completely on the subject at hand.
- *Don't* ignore the idea of layers and channels when you feel overwhelmed and frustrated.

Take Action

1. Set aside a few minutes each week to review your various channels and decide how you'll address issues that can and will arise.
2. Discuss the idea of a "wall of happiness" with a trusted person. Identify the bricks that each of you want to place to build your own walls.

Appendix I: Summary of Ideas, Related Actions, *Stoppers*, and Strategies

Aristotle's guidance can assist you in your quest for happiness. The goal is to lead a virtuous life—not only knowing the right thing to do but doing the right thing, at the right time, for the right person, and in the right way.

There are 10 ideas of Aristotle's philosophy you can apply to assist in your active pursuit of happiness. However, significant barriers or *stoppers* can interfere with your efforts. Being acutely aware of both the 10 ideas and the *stoppers* helps you plan and then take action. In addition, you can apply three strategies to become more efficient in your efforts.

This chapter reviews the ideas, actions, *stoppers*, and strategies you need to know as you pursue happiness in a succinct summary.

10 Ideas and Related Actions

Idea #1: Happiness is an activity or a state actualized by an activity.

Action: *Embrace the notion that something must be done for happiness.* Happiness is not a state in the sense that a coma is a state; it is an activity or a state actualized by action or activity. You must take action for happiness. It will not come knocking on your door.

Idea #2: Each person needs to accept responsibility for the actions and judgments he or she takes.
Action: *Embrace responsibility for your actions, even when you might fail.* In the short term, you might be pained. In the long term you have a better chance for happiness.

Idea #3: The Theory of the Mean is Aristotle's tool to help deliberate about excess and deficiency. One should seek the mean between excess and deficiency to find balance and identify actions that are appropriate (virtuous) in the course of everyday life.
Action: *Continually determine your proximity to the mean* with all of your actions. According to Aristotle, your ability to reason well is a critical part of being intelligent. Be thoughtful about the entirety of your life. Because excellence is found within the whole of your life, no specific aspect should dominate.

Idea #4: There is no single end—such as accomplishment, fame, or fortune—that assures happiness.
Action: *Abandon the idea of a single goal or dominant end.* When you seek happiness, identify a variety or multiplicity of ends, and focus on virtuous action.

Idea #5: Rational thought and reason can help you control emotional responses and make balanced decisions.
Action: *Control your emotions with the use of reason.* Diminish or avoid emotional decision-making. Because impulse (or emotion) isn't conducive to happiness, allow time to calm your emotions, think about the situation and possible consequences, and then create a plan.

Idea #6: Even the most prosperous can fail. There is no insurance or guarantee of stability.

Action: *Hope for the best but plan for the worst.* When change or failure occurs, understand that there's always a new day and new opportunity to do the right thing.

Idea #7: Happiness is comprised of a multiplicity of ends. It is the actions you take when pursuing these ends that provide the basis for a happy life.

Action: *Purge the unrealistic expectation that when a particular need is satisfied, happiness will occur.*

Idea #8: An intelligent person *knows* the right thing to do, in the right way, at the right time, and for the right reason.

Action: *To experience true intelligence, learn to deliberate well about the correct action to take for you and others.* Intelligence is more than learning facts.

Idea #9: An excellent person *does* the right thing, in the right way, at the right time, and for the right reason.

Action: *Remember to take action once you are aware of what needs to be done.* Avoid seduction by more immediate and attractive options that come your way.

Idea #10: Happiness is continuing general life satisfaction, not satisfaction with all things at all times.

Action: *Continuously evaluate and reevaluate using rational thought to find balance.* Answer a question such as "What is the right thing to do at this time?"

Stoppers

Chapter 1: Happiness: A *stopper* can occur (a) because of a lack of knowledge about how to achieve happiness, (b) when thoughts or actions are compelled by emotion rather than rational thought, or (c) as a result of inaction. You need to take certain kinds of action to achieve happiness—that is, doing the right thing, for the right person, at the right time, in the right way, and for the right reason.

Chapter 2: Responsibility: A *stopper* can occur as a result of (a) denying personal responsibility in order to avoid the negative consequences of your actions, (b) telling lies, which erodes trust and is destructive to sound decision making, or (c) refusing to embrace responsibility. When you embrace responsibility, you move from emotionally defending yourself to actively participating in rational problem solving.

Chapter 3: Fame and Fortune: *Stoppers* develop when you (a) fail to differentiate between success and happiness, (b) focus on money, success, or fame, (c) pursue being honored as opposed to being honorable, (d) accept recognition for undeserved or trivial accomplishments, (e) pursue one dominant end (or goal), (f) overemphasize the importance of winning, or (g) think it's important to have power over others.

Chapter 4: Balance: *Stoppers* can occur when you (a) commit to one dominant end to the exclusion of all others, (b) fail to find the balance between excess and deficiency, or (c) confuse short-term pleasant emotional responses (pleasure) with continuing life satisfaction (happiness).

Chapter 5: Unrealistic Expectations: *Stoppers* can occur when you (a) suffer unnecessary disappointment from unrealistic expectations, (b) suffer unnecessary disappointment from expecting good results when you do the right thing for the wrong reason, (c) think having fun is what brings happiness, when in reality, relaxation is a preparation for serious thought and action, or (d) think your good reputation precedes you.

Chapter 6: Change and Failure: *Stoppers* can emerge when you (a) resist life's inevitable changes and failures, (b) ignore clues about negative developments in your life, (c) confuse effective optimism with pessimism, or (d) use sledgehammer words, a practice that triggers emotion and reduces rational thought.

Chapter 7: Irresolvable Problems: *Stoppers* arise when you (a) deny the existence of unchangeable relationships, (b) deny your mortality, (c) allow yourself to be overwhelmed when faced with what appear to be irresolvable problems, (d) deny the opportunity to understand how a different perspective or philosophic assumption can help solve a problem, or (e) deny happiness is attainable even when your situation changes for the worse.

Chapter 8: Steps toward Happiness: *Stoppers* that result from being overwhelmed can occur when you neglect to (a) create a separate channel for each aspect of your life, (b) work on a multiplicity of ends in your life, and (c) visualize each end as a brick in your wall of happiness.

3 Strategies

Strategy #1: The concept of layers and channels is a tool to help organize one's thoughts and meet challenges. The idea of layers and channels is consistent with Aristotle's contention that multiple ends help build your "wall of happiness."

Action: Build channels in your mind to reduce feeling overwhelmed by life circumstances. Assist your reason in ruling your emotions by dealing with one issue at a time.

Strategy #2: The "wall of happiness" provides an image of the "big picture" of your life over time and facilitates your ability to achieve one thing at a time (one brick at a time).

Action: Remember the aspects of your life that you value. Think of each aspect as an important brick in your "wall of happiness." None of these bricks, no matter how important they are individually, is—or can be—a wall. Rather, each is subordinate to the wall and part of the totality.

Strategy #3: Focus on the ways you can take charge of your happiness (1) by using your *true intelligence* to find the right thing to do, and (2) striving for *excellence* by doing the right thing, for the right person, at the right time, and in the right way.

Action: Schedule specific times to think about the values you cherish, and then create mental images of ways you can have more experiences based on those values.

Appendix II: Applying Aristotle's Ideas to Life Dilemmas

How Would You Deal with This Situation?

When life presents dilemmas, it helps to reflect on these issues and discuss ways to do the right thing, in the right way, to the right person, and in the right way.

Here are situations that relate to the information provided in each chapter. If these examples aren't relevant to you, consider identifying other issues to discuss with colleagues, friends, or family.

Chapter 1: Happiness: Imagine you're a student in an advanced mathematics seminar. You have developed enough of a relationship with your professor to know something about her. She graduated with a doctoral degree from Harvard. A brilliant scholar, she's earned international awards in mathematics. However, you know she's had personal difficulties with many students and faculty members and seems to look unhappy. In a moment of weakness, she insists she's happy but would like to be happier.

Considering what you have read in Chapter 1, how would you respond to the following statements made by your professor?

- "To be intelligent, you need to be able to collect and analyze complicated facts and theories."
- "Businesspeople are intelligent if they are shrewd."

- "Reason is more important than emotions in making judgments."
- "A solid background in the sciences is the best preparation for making major life decisions."
- "Sometimes I'm happy, and sometimes I'm not."
- "I'm happy, but I'd like to be happier."
- "What I need to do to be happy is just a matter of opinion."

Chapter 2: Responsibility: Imagine you are an attorney. The firm's most important client calls to say you've missed an important filing, thereby putting the ruling on his case in jeopardy. Quite a bit of money is involved. The client says *you* are responsible for this potential loss. Yet you're sure the client did not respond to your last request for information when you warned him about the potential of this problem. You experience a rush of emotions and ask yourself a bunch of "what ifs" including, "What if the case goes to litigation?" Although you think your errors and omissions will be covered by insurance, it doesn't matter. Regardless of your fear of failure or humiliation, your most critical focus is retaining the firm's client. Still, the client insists that he didn't receive anything from you about this matter and claims again your responsibility for this mess. Although you're worried, you need to move into problem solving. In the meantime, the client requests a meeting with your managing partner.

Based on what you read in Chapter 2, what do you think your best action would be? Explain why.

- Tell the client he didn't respond to your last memo; if he had done so, there would be no problem.
- Tell the client you will check the file and get back to him.

- Take responsibility and immediately apologize for whatever part you played in creating the problem. Suggest working toward an action plan for a solution and offer to bring in the managing partner if you cannot help solve the problem.
- Make sure everyone knows this incident was the result of moral luck.
- Tell a "little white lie" to buy some time, saying there's no problem so don't worry; the missed filing is meaningless.

Chapter 3: Fame and Fortune: Barney, an outstanding athlete in his junior year of college, is a contender for the Heisman Trophy. He recently received a multimillion-dollar offer to play professional football. Accepting the offer would require Barney to quit school immediately. He says, "I've already been honored. This offer is my chance to be rich and famous. If I accept, my family and I will be financially secure and *happy* for the rest of our lives. If I pass on this chance for happiness, I may never get it again. I could even get injured in my last college season and lose everything. Therefore, I'm quitting school and signing that contract."

Having grown up in a poor family, Barney expects his parents to enthusiastically support this decision to sign the contract. To his surprise, his parents respond by saying, "Finish school before you attempt to make it as a professional. Whatever honors you have received are a matter of the past. You overestimate the importance of being rich, and you completely misunderstand and overvalue being famous. Receiving honors and being rich and famous aren't all they're cracked up to be. Your happiness doesn't depend on these things."

Based on what you've read in this book, how would you respond to the following questions?

- Do you think it's obvious what Barney should do?
- How do you think Barney should evaluate his decision?
- What would you say about Barney's view of happiness?
- What do you think of Barney's view of fame?
- What do you think of the views expressed by Barney's parents?
- Do you think Barney's parents are naïve?
- How would you value the honors Barney has received in the past?

Chapter 4: Balance: Harry works long hours and never seems available for his children's activities or family matters. He seems completely focused on getting ahead in his firm and making more money. Harry defends himself by saying he's working for the good of the family, their private school tuitions, and all the other benefits they've struggled hard to realize. When they're honest with themselves, Noreen and Harry both agree that their family life is out of balance; they feel trapped by the lifestyle they've created for themselves. Their two children, though, love their private schools and the lifestyle they've come to expect. What would you advise Noreen and Harry to do in this circumstance?

- Is this dilemma simply a matter of choosing, or is this couple really stuck?
- Is it just dreaming to think about selling everything and moving to a simpler life, or would it be practical?
- Do Harry and Noreen have an obligation to their children to continue the life they've been "promised"?
- Would Noreen and Harry be unhappy no matter what lifestyle they had chosen?

Chapter 5: Unrealistic Expectations: Your cousin, Frank, who's out of work and broke, has always been helpful to you and the rest of the family. Being close, he expects you to provide him with financial assistance. As it happens, your finances are good so you lend him a substantial amount of money. He said he'd repay it in a year.

Frank takes the money but seems disappointed. He says, "You know, it's not a loan I expected from you. I expected meaningful financial relief. In some sense," he adds, "if I have to repay this loan in a year, it makes the problem worse."

With a trace of bitterness, Frank reminds you of the many times he's helped you over the years—like taking care of the children when you were sick. Because of that, he expects more from you in his moment of need. Frank's disappointment leads to trouble. He stops communicating with you about anything, including the money. He doesn't repay the loan, and he remains out of work. You feel disappointed in Frank.

Based on what you've read in this book, how would you respond to the following questions?

- Did Frank have unrealistic expectations?
- Did you have unrealistic expectations?
- What would you say to Frank regarding this situation?
- Do you think you made a bad decision in lending the money to Frank?
- How might you have avoided this problem with Frank?

Chapter 6: Change and Failure: Your friend Gabriella, a seasoned and successful speaker, says, "I failed miserably at my last presentation. My colleague had warned me to be careful at least two weeks before the meeting, saying the vice president responsible for planning these events had been replaced. The new vice president, assigned to reviewing all the presenters, was committed to making changes—perhaps with negative consequences for me. I thought my colleague was being overly pessimistic. After all, I've been leading this kind of seminar successfully for twenty years. It seemed to me nothing would be different. Because of this thinking, I didn't pursue the matter with my client. Consequently, I didn't understand exactly what changes the new vice president wanted. What happened? I made a mess of things and lost my biggest client. The vice president blamed me for the failed session and terminated my engagement for the rest of the planned seminars. I guess I'm no longer qualified to do this kind of work. The worst professional mistake I have ever made resulted in a humiliating failure—one I might never get over."

Based on what you read in this chapter, which how would you respond to the following comments made by Gabriella?

- "The problem was unavoidable. The new VP was determined to make changes."
- "Maybe I was afraid to hear what the new VP would say I had to do."
- "It was unethical for my client to change the person I report to without notifying me."
- "I've been doing presentations successfully for twenty years. I know how to do them. I cannot believe they would do this to me."
- "My colleague is always looking for trouble ahead. She's too pessimistic for our business to grow."
- "If this the way people are going to treat me, I can't do this anymore."

Chapter 7: Irresolvable Problems: Your retailer friend Tim tells you he's in despair because the company he founded thirty years ago is in great danger of failing in the near future. Big box stores opening in his area can sell for less than he can buy. He knows that unavoidable trouble is coming, but it's hard to face. On top of his business problems, his kids are in trouble. His daughter is on scholastic probation at the university, and his son's marriage is deteriorating—irresolvable problems in his mind. He'll never be able to compete with the big box stores, and he isn't in control of his own grown children.

Based on what you read in this and other chapters, how would you respond to the following questions?

- Is Tim correct to say some of his problems are irresolvable?
- Is Tim responsible for any or all of these problems?
- Is it rational for Tim to be surprised at his lack of control?
- Could Tim have predicted some the problems he has?
- Is it accurate to call Tim's disappointment with his son and daughter an *irresolvable* problem?

Chapter 8: Steps toward Happiness: Lauren is a gifted, financially disadvantaged, and overwhelmed high school student. She's pressured to keep her grades up while also preparing for the ACT and SAT college admissions examinations. In addition, she's struggling to hold her starting position on the field hockey team and continue her volunteer work. Lauren thinks that, with enough effort, she can win a top spot in the science fair, thus enhancing her chances of a needed scholarship. Lauren says that, although she feels overwhelmed, she can't stop or change anything.

Based on what you've read in this chapter, how would you respond to a student like Lauren if she were to make the following statements?

- "I can do a number of things at the same time."
- "Everything on my plate is of equal importance."
- "I have so many things to do that I can't seem to completely focus on anything."
- "If I just discipline myself, I can do all of this and more."
- "I feel overwhelmed."

Appendix III: Applying Aristotle's Ideas as Your Personal Action Guide

How Have I Taken Action? How Will I Take Action?

The following activities help you reflect and record your reactions to the thoughts presented in each chapter. When you have a structured format, you can engage in self-dialogue and move between the past, present, and future perspectives. You use your rational mind to identify your strengths and ways to deal with *stoppers* to happiness.

Chapter 1: Happiness:

Happiness is described as continued life satisfaction, not satisfaction with everything all the time. A lack of awareness of your happiness status can be a *stopper* to attaining happiness. Reflect upon your current perception of happiness. Rate your general life satisfaction using a scale from 1 to 10, with 10 representing the greatest level of satisfaction.

Your Happiness Self-Check				
	Low 1–3	Moderate 4–6	High 7–10	Comments
General Life				
Work				
Home				
Other				

Review your rating and ask, “How do I view my life happiness? Does it vary, depending on the setting?”

In the past, have you viewed happiness differently than you do now, depending on the circumstance? For example, if you were sick or in severe financial crisis, did you think happiness would result if the illness or financial crisis passed? Describe the situation and lessons you learned about happiness.

Aristotle’s distinction between intelligence and excellence is one that demands reflection—especially when what you know you should do is different from the action you take. Too often, although you may have insight and knowledge about the right thing to do, you might not take the action required to do it.

Use this chart to record times/situations in which you felt intelligent, excellent, or neither.

Self-Check: Intelligence and Excellence

	Intelligent	Excellent	Neither	Comments
Time/ Situation:				
Work				
Home				
Other				

Review your notes and ask, "How often do I know the right thing to do, but not do it? Do I tend to be excellent in one situation rather than another? In what ways might I move toward consistently taking action that accords with what I know I should do?—that is, even when I don't want to do it."

To live a virtuous life and enjoy continued life satisfaction, you must use rational thinking rather than emotions to make decisions. Reflect upon the persons, places, or events where you are most likely to act with emotion rather than rational thought. After you jot some notes, ask questions like "Do my emotions sometimes present *stoppers* to a satisfying life? In what ways can I consider altering my feelings and reactions?"

Self-Check: Emotional and Rational Thinking

	Emotional Thinking	Rational Thinking	*Stopper*	Comments
Time/ Situation				
Work				
Home				
Other				

Review your notes and ask, "How often do emotions, rather than rational thinking, dictate my behavior? Do I tend to depend on rational thinking more in one kind of situation rather than another? In what ways might I move toward relying on rational thought in my decision making or other behavior?'

Chapter 2: Responsibility

When you deny your responsibility for the road you travel (or have traveled) or your role in a failure, then a *stopper* emerges that can thwart your pursuit of happiness.

Reflect upon the way you deal with responsibility, given your role at work, home, or other settings. On the next page rate the level to which you accept responsibility. Use a scale from 1 to 10, with 10 representing the highest level.

Self-Check: Responsibility at Work and Home

Setting	Role	Low 1–3	Moderate 4–6	High 7–10	Comments
Work	Leader				
	Team Member				
	Independent Professional				
Home	Spouse/ Partner				
	Parent/ Grandparent				
	Other Family				
Other					

Review your rating. Ask, "Do I tend to accept responsibility differently, depending on the setting? In what ways should I consider acting in a more consistent manner?" Note the persons, places, and events that might be affected if you could revise your tendency to accept or deny responsibility.

Chapter 3: Fame and Fortune

Although some level of material well-being is required for happiness, when you overestimate the meaningfulness of money or success, you can create *stoppers* that can block your happiness.

Think about those you know who have won awards, honors, or fortunes. What has happened to these people? What positive benefits did they see because of the honors or awards? What, if anything, can be learned from what you have seen?

Worksheet: Persons and Awards

Persons	Award	Your Reaction	Long-term/ Short-term Benefits

Chapter 4: Balance

According to Aristotle, it takes a multiplicity of ends to find happiness because no one factor is sufficient for happiness. The Theory of the Mean provides a tool for finding the mean between excess and deficiency for any particular factor.

Consider Aristotle's Theory of the Mean. Refer to the columns below. There are ten rows of characteristics in each column. Along the left side, there is a list of deficiencies. Along the right, there is a list of excesses. In the middle column is the word describing the mean between deficiency and excess for each characteristic? On the next page rate yourself as to where you fit for each characteristic. Skip a characteristic if it lacks relevance for you. A rating of 1 or 2 indicates deficiency, while a rating of 9 or 10 indicates excess.

Self-Check: The Mean Between Excess and Deficiency		
Vice of Deficiency	**Mean**	**Vice of Excess**
Fearfulness	**Courage**	Overconfidence
Insensibility	**Temperance**	Self-indulgence
Stinginess	**Generosity**	Wasteful recklessness
False humility	**High-mindedness**	Excessive pride
Lacking in ambition	**Right ambition**	Overly ambitious
Spiritless	**Even tempered**	Volatile
Quarrelsomeness and surliness	**Friendly civility**	Excessive flattering
Disingenuousness	**Sincerity**	Excessive frankness
Chronic seriousness	**Wittiness**	Undignified levity
Shame at nothing	**Modesty**	Shame at everything

Review your ratings: if you are living according to Aristotle's Theory of the Mean, then your ratings fall in the 4 to 6 range. If your scores indicate a lack of balance in any major areas of your life, think about what corrective action you might take.

1. Can you identify people in your life who seem to have achieved balance? Spend some time speaking with them, and try to identify the virtuous activities in which they participate.
2. Visualize your life as it is now. List the ends that you are pursuing. Describe the obstacles to reaching each of your goals.

Worksheet: Goals and Possible *Stoppers*

Goals	**Possible Obstacles or *Stoppers***
1.	
2.	
3	
4.	
5.	

Review the obstacles/*stoppers* and ask, "How have these factors inhibited my happiness in previous years? What changes can I consider to reduce the effect of these *stoppers*?"

Chapter 5: Unrealistic Expectations

You remove a potential *stopper* to happiness when you avoid unrealistic expectations. For example, do not expect reciprocation for your good acts or expect that some experience, such as going to a good school, having a life of leisure, or winning the lottery, will result in happiness.

Select two stages of your life, and describe some of your expectations during this time. Note ways in which you were and were not realistic.

Worksheet: Expectations and Related Consequences

Stage	What Did I Expect?	In What Ways Were the Expectations Realistic or Unrealistic?	What Were the Results or Comments?

Review the unrealistic expectations, and ask, "How have these factors inhibited my happiness in previous years? What changes can I consider to reduce the effect of these *stoppers*?"

Chapter 6: Change and Failure

Change is a continuing and inevitable life condition. It is often upsetting to people, and they may deny or ignore the clues of impending changes. Resisting change is a potential *stopper* to happiness. Review a few stages of your life, identify times or situations in which you denied or resisted change, and reflect on how it affected your happiness?

Worksheet: Life Stages and Changes

Life Stage	When, Where, and with Whom Did You Deny or Resist Change?	What Was the Result and How Did You Feel about It?
Childhood		
Adolescence		
Young Adulthood		
Adulthood		
Senior		

Review your notes and ask, "How has denial of change inhibited my happiness in previous years? What changes can I consider to reduce the effects of these *stoppers*?"

Reflect upon the way you deal with failure or the fear of it, given your role at work, home, or another setting. Rate the level to which you effectively deal with failure. Use a scale from 1 to 10, with 10 representing the most effectiveness in dealing with failure.

Worksheet: Dealing with Failure

Role	What Did I Expect?	In What Ways Were the Expectations Realistic or Unrealistic?	What Were the Results or Comments?
Work			
Home			
Other			

Review your rating. Ask, "Do I tend to deal with possible or real failure differently, depending on the setting? In what ways should I consider acting in a more consistent manner?" Note the persons, places, and events that would be affected if you could revise the manner in which you deal with real or potential failure.

Chapter 7: Irresolvable Problems

Describe ways you have thought about your own mortality at different stages of your life. When did you start to think about your own mortality? Does an awareness of your mortality change the way in which you conduct your life? Does it change the way you view death?

Worksheet: Life Stages and Views of Mortality

	How Often Did/Do You Think about Your Own Mortality?	What Were/Are Your Reactions To Mortality?
Childhood		
Adolescence		
Young Adulthood		
Adulthood		
Senior		

Review your views about mortality and ask, "How has this factor inhibited my happiness in previous years? What changes can I consider to increase my satisfaction with life?"

Chapter 8: Steps toward Happiness

Aristotle advises that thoughtfulness and action are required for happiness. The concepts and images of layers and channels and the wall of happiness are two ways that can help you understand problems and devise solutions.

Use the spaces below to name some of the channels of your life. A channel might be about a family member, financial issue, professional problem, medical problem, disagreement, lawsuit, etc. List the obstacles that might cause you to "layer up" and lose focus. List the actions that you can take to overcome the obstacles in order to improve your focus.

Channel One: ____________________________________

- Obstacles to focusing:

- Actions that will help me overcome obstacles:

Channel Two: ____________________________________

- Obstacles to focusing:

- Actions that will help me overcome obstacles:

Channel Three: ______________________________

- Obstacles to focusing:

- Actions that will help me overcome obstacles:

Visualize your wall of happiness. In each square or "brick," write the name of a critical aspect or person in your life that you want/ need to focus on.

Review your notes and reflect about ways that you can maintain those behaviors and actions that build your wall and change those that present *stoppers.*

Your Action Plan: Moving from *Knowing* the Right Thing to *Doing* the Right Thing

How can you move toward greater, sustained satisfaction in life? What can you do to enjoy a state of well-being and contentment? As a starting point, happiness requires the commitment to a certain kind of life. Identifying and doing the right thing will lead you in the right direction. Make a plan and execute it. Any rational plan will do. The simplest plan is often the best plan. You act, see what works and what doesn't, and then adjust. Find the *stoppers,* and revise your plan. You have a continuous cycle of action and adaptation. Use the following chart to get started. After completing the chart, schedule your actions on your calendar and find a family member or friend with whom to share your progress.

Worksheet: Doing the Right Thing

Situation	The Right Thing to Do	Possible *Stopper*(s)	What You Need to Say to Yourself	What You Need to Do
1.				
2.				
3.				

Appendix IV: Discussion Questions or Book Club Guide

Use the following discussion questions to guide your thinking or book club activities.

Chapter 1: Happiness

1. What are the differences between the definition of *intelligence* used by Aristotle and the definition used by the general population?
2. Who in your professional or personal life exemplifies Aristotle's concept of the *intelligent*, but not *excellent* person?
3. Who in your professional or personal life exemplifies Aristotle's concept of an *excellent* person?
4. Can you think of circumstances when you knew what the right thing to do was, but you did not act on it?
5. In what ways can you use Aristotle's view of the rational mind for practical ethical issues?

Chapter 2: Responsibility

1. Describe a situation in which you were responsible for an error but denied or avoided responsibility.
2. What is the relationship, if any, between taking responsibility and finding happiness?

3. Give an example of a "little white lie" you have told. What is the harm in what some people characterize as meaningless "little white lies"?
4. Do you think it's sometimes wise to overstate your accomplishments or the accomplishments of your children? Specify how you have overstated and to whom. If you have examples, are you regretful?
5. Describe what you think of someone when you think he or she has lied. Describe any difference in your answer between "small lies" and lies of omission.

Chapter 3: Fame and Fortune

1. What can a rich and famous person (e.g., a movie star) do to maintain a balanced life while surrounded by what appears to be meaningless excess?
2. Describe people you know who focus on "goods of the soul."
3. Why do you think people are so often envious of the rich and famous even when faced with evidence they are not happy?
4. What thoughts do you have when others receive awards that you hoped to win?
5. In what ways does it matter to you whether your peers recognize you for a job well done?
6. In what way do you think the awarding of recognition, overall, works to our societal advantage?

Chapter 4: Balance

1. How do you think the time and effort spent meeting your primary duties to be successful inevitably lead to an unbalanced life?

2. Do you try to make decisions and take actions based on "a mean between two extremes"?
3. Can you think of a difficult moment when, under pressure, you did the right thing?
4. Who are the people in your life who seem to be out of balance?
5. Why do you think it is so difficult to live a balanced life?

Chapter 5: Unrealistic Expectations

1. Did you receive the benefits you expected from your education or training?
2. To what degree has your professional life been fulfilling or disappointing?
3. Have you been generous, both financially and ethically? Has your generosity yielded what you expected?
4. Have you had disappointments resulting from your unrealized expectations? For example, were there unrealized expectations about your children or other family members? Have these disappointments had a negative effect on your happiness?

Chapter 6: Change and Failure

1. Do you know anyone who seems to be good at finding clues in his or her environment? How does this ability help him or her in their personal and professional planning?
2. Does the lack of precise information inhibit you from deciding what to do?
3. If the answer to #2 is yes, What can you say to yourself to better confront change or failure?
4. In what ways can you use the Theory of the Mean as a tool to help you deal with failure?

5. Can you describe a personal failure that unexpectedly led to a good result?

Chapter 7: Irresolvable Problems

1. How do you think you should respond to others when they treat you badly?
2. Do you think suicide is ever the excellent thing to do? In what circumstances?
3. In what way do you think having a permanent awareness of your own mortality can help you more toward happiness?
4. Describe circumstances when you have been confronted with perceived irresolvable problems.
5. Describe any situations where you used philosophical concepts to help you with personal or professional problems.

Chapter 8: Steps toward Happiness

1. We all know people who seem to manage all their relationships and issues effectively, always focusing on the moment. What are they doing to manage their channels and avoid layering?
2. What can you learn by looking around you? Is there someone you know who might benefit from using a tool like layers and channels?
3. In what ways can you use the concept of layers and channels as a tool for the management of your own life?
4. In what ways can you use the concept of a wall of happiness as a tool for the management of your own life?
5. What are issues in your life that require a greater and more pinpointed focus in order for you to attain happiness?

References and Recommended Reading

Ackrill, J. L. 1981. *Aristotle the Philosopher.* Oxford, England: Clarendon Press.

Aristotle. 1985. *Nicomachean Ethics.* Translated by Terence Irwin. Indianapolis, IN: Hackett Publishing Company.

Ben-Shahar, T. 2007. *Happier: Learn the Secrets to Daily Joy and Lasting Fulfillment.* New York: McGraw-Hill Companies.

Blakeslee, S. 2001. "Car Calls May Leave Brain Short-Handed." *The New York Times,* July 31. http://www.nytimes.com/2001/.../car-calls-may-leave-brain-short-handed.html

Carlson, R. 2006. *You Can Be Happy No Matter What: Five Principles for Keeping Life in Perspective.* Novato, CA: New World Library.

Cave, D. 2010. "In Recession, Americans Doing More, Buying Less." *The New York Times,* Jan. 2. http://www.nytimes.com/2010/01/03/business/economy/03experience.html.

Chopra, D. 2009. The *Ultimate Happiness Prescription: 7 Keys to Joy and Enlightenment.* New York: Harmony Books.

Csikszentmihalyi, M. 2008. *Flow: The Psychology of Optimal Experience.* New York: HarperCollins Publishers.

Foster, R., and G. Hicks. 1999. *How We Choose to Be Happy.* New York: G. P. Putnam.

Fredrickson, B. L. 2009. *Positivity: Top-Notch Research Reveals the 3-to-1 Factor That Will Change Your Life.* New York: Three Rivers Press.

Frost, Robert. 1920. "The Road Not Taken." *Mountain Interval.* New York: Henry Holt and Company.

Gandhi, M. 1993. *An Autobiography: The Story of My Experiments with Truth.* Boston, MA: Beacon Press.

Gentry, W. D. 2008. *Happiness for Dummies.* Hoboken, N.J.: Wiley Publishers.

Gilbert, D. 2005. *Stumbling on Happiness.* New York: Vintage Books.

Haidt, J. 2006. *The Happiness Hypothesis: Finding Modern Truth in Ancient Wisdom.* New York: Basic Books.

Heidegger, M. 1962. *Being and Time.* New York: Harper & Row.

Kameneu, M. 2006. "Rating Countries for the Happiness Factor." http://www.businessweek.com/globalbiz/content /RatingCountriesfortheHappinessFactor ct2006 /gb20061011_072596.htm

Kushner, H. S. 1981. *When Bad Things Happen to Good People.* New York: Anchor.

Lama, D., and H. C. Cutler. 2009. *The Art of Happiness in a Troubled World.* New York: Random House.

Lyubomirsky, S. 2008. *The How of Happiness: A Scientific Approach to Getting the Life You Want.* New York: Penguin Press.

Marinoff, L. 2000. *Plato, Not Prozac! Applying Eternal Wisdom to Everyday Problems.* New York: Harper Perennial.

McKeon, R. 1941. *The Basic Works of Aristotle.* New York: Random House.

Meltzer, Mark. 2000. *Lottery Winners Often Wind up Wishing They Hadn't Been Lucky.* Notebook, *Atlanta Business Chronicle.* http:atlanta.bizjournals.com/Atlanta/stories/2000/05/22 /editorial1.html

Myers, D. G. 1992. *The Pursuit of Happiness: Discovering the Pathway to Fulfillment, Well-Being, and Enduring Personal Joy.* New York: Avon.

Nagel, T. 1979. *Moral Questions.* Cambridge, England: Cambridge University Press.

Peale, N. V. 1980. *The Power of Positive Thinking.* New York: Fireside.

Person, C. 2006. *A Primer in Positive Psychology.* New York: University Press.

Pew Research Center. 2006. http://pewresearch.org/pubs/301/are-we-happy-yet

Prager, D. 1999. *Happiness is a Serious Problem: A Human Nature Repair Manual.* New York: Harper Perennial.

Rubin, G. 2009. *The Happiness Project.* New York: HarperCollins.

Rubinstein, J. D., D. E. Meyer, and J. E. Evans. 2001. "Executive Control of Cognitive Processes in Task Switching." *Journal of Experimental Psychology: Human Perception and Performance* 27/4:763–797.

Ryan, S. 2008. *A Look at Famous Lottery Winners.* http//www.hellium.com/items/841985-a-look-at-famous -lottery-winners 10/13/08

Seligman, M. E. P. 1991. *Learned Optimism.* New York: Knopf.

________. 2002. *Authentic Happiness: Using the New Positive Psychology to Realize Your Potential for Lasting Fulfillment.* New York: Free Press.

________. 2010. *Flourish: A Visionary New Understanding of Happiness and Well-being.* New York: Simon & Schuster.

Wesley, M. 2007. "More Sad Stories Of Lottery Winners Ending Up Broke, Depressed and Lonely." Life Midlife Improvement. http://lifetwo.com/production/node/20070425-more-sad -stories-of-lottery-winners-ending-up-broke-depressed-and -lonely

Williams, B. 1983. *Moral Luck.* Cambridge, England: Cambridge University Press.
Witters, D. 2011. Americans Happier, Less Stressed in 2010. Gallup Poll. http://www.gallup.com/poll/145457/americans-happier-less-stressed-2010.aspx

About the Authors

Gary Madvin, CLU, ChFC, is the founder of Financial Management Services (FMS Financial Partners, Inc.), a financial planning firm in Los Angeles, California. He is a college lecturer and self-help seminar leader. He is also a consultant to companies interested in international distribution and development. Discover more information and strategies at www.happinesswitharistotle.com or contact Gary Madvin at garymadvin@happinesswitharistotle.com.

Geraldine Markel, PhD, is principal of Managing Your Mind Coaching & Seminars. She is an educational psychologist, former faculty at the School of Education, University of Michigan, and author of several books on learning and productivity. Her most recent book is, "Defeating the Demons of Distraction: Proven Strategies to Increase Productivity and Decrease Stress". For additional information, contact gerimarkel@happinesswitharistotle.com

Index

V

W

Made in the USA
Las Vegas, NV
04 February 2022

43090448R00100